A CATSKILL WOODSMAN
MIKE TODD'S STORY

A CATSKILL WOODSMAN

Mike Todd's Story

as told to

Norman Studer

PURPLE MOUNTAIN PRESS
Fleischmanns, New York

The publisher gratefully acknowledges the editorial advise of
Eve Fairbairn Budd and the assistance of Edwin Doremus, Saralyn Esh,
Janet Allison and Patty Kelly

Photographs courtesy of Betty Baker and Stuart Gross

Photograph of Norman Studer by Herbert Haufrecht

First published by Purple Mountain Press in 1988
Second printing: November 1988
Third printing: May 1997

Please note: A reader of the first edition pointed out that Mike Todd might have confused the names of the murderer and the murdered on page 105.

Copyright © 1988 by Joan Studer Levine

All rights reserved under International and Pan-American Copyright Conventions. No part of this book may be reproduced or transmitted in any form without permission in writing from the publisher.

PURPLE MOUNTAIN PRESS, LTD.
Main Street, P.O. Box E3, Fleischmanns, New York 12430-0378
914-254-4062, 914-254-4476 (fax)

Library of Congress Cataloging-in-Publication Data

Todd, Mike, 1877-1960.
    A Catskill woodsman : Mike Todd's story / as told to Norman Studer.
    p.   cm.
    Includes index.
    ISBN 0-935796-08-8 (pbk.)
    1. Todd, Mike, 1877-1969. 2. Catskill Mountains (N.Y.)- -Social life and customs. 3. Catskill Mountains (N.Y.)- -Biography.
4. Mountain life- -New York (State)- -Catskill Mountains.
5. Storytellers- -New York (State)- -Catskill Mountains- -Biography.
I. Studer, Norman. II. Title.
[F127.C3T63   1997]
974.7'38043'092- -dc21
  [B]   97-14289
                                                              CIP

Manufactured in the United States of America

TABLE OF CONTENTS

DEDICATION	1
INTRODUCTION	3
EARLY YEARS	11
BORN A HUNTER	28
MUSIC EDUCATION	33
A STORY-TELLER'S EDUCATION	36
LIFE OF A POACHER	39
A FUGITIVE IN PENNSYLVANIA	46
ON THE TOWER	57
MR. BEAR OF THE CATSKILLS	72
WOMEN IN HIS LIFE	81
SKILLS OF A WOODSMAN	83
TOO OLD TO WORK	88
YARNS OF A CATSKILL WOODSMAN	91
"STOP THIS BEAR HUNT"	107
THE LAST YEARS	110
A REAL MOUNTAIN MAN	112
NOTES	115
INDEX	119

The publisher gratefully acknowledges the editorial advise of
Eve Fairbairn Budd and the assistance of Edwin Doremus, Saralyn Esh,
Janet Allison and Patty Kelly

Photographs courtesy of Betty Baker and Stuart Gross

Photograph of Norman Studer by Herbert Haufrecht

First published by Purple Mountain Press in 1988
Second printing: November 1988
Third printing: May 1997

Please note: A reader of the first edition pointed out that Mike Todd might
have confused the names of the murderer and the murdered on page 105.

Copyright © 1988 by Joan Studer Levine

All rights reserved under International and Pan-American Copyright
Conventions. No part of this book may be reproduced or transmitted in
any form without permission in writing from the publisher.

PURPLE MOUNTAIN PRESS, LTD.
Main Street, P.O. Box E3, Fleischmanns, New York 12430-0378
914-254-4062, 914-254-4476 (fax)

Library of Congress Cataloging-in-Publication Data

Todd, Mike, 1877-1960.
    A Catskill woodsman : Mike Todd's story / as told to Norman
Studer.
       p.   cm.
    Includes index.
    ISBN 0-935796-08-8 (pbk.)
    1. Todd, Mike, 1877-1969. 2. Catskill Mountains (N.Y.)- -Social
life and customs. 3. Catskill Mountains (N.Y.)- -Biography.
4. Mountain life- -New York (State)- -Catskill Mountains.
5. Storytellers- -New York (State)- -Catskill Mountains- -Biography.
I. Studer, Norman. II. Title.
[F127.C3T63   1997]
974.7'38043'092- -dc21
[B]   97-14289
                                                                        CIP

Manufactured in the United States of America

DEDICATION

This book is Norman Studer's memorial to Mike Todd. At the same time, it is a modest monument to himself—one of the many legacies of his life in the Catskills. One of his last requests, a little more than a week before he died, was that I take a photo of Mike's tombstone for inclusion in this book. Norman was still happily preoccupied with the recording and continuance of the folk tradition.
If he were alive today, I know Norman would dedicate this book to the memory of Mike Todd and all the other story-tellers, folk singers and musicians of the Catskills with whom he forged lasting friendships. He had a great way of bringing out and publicizing their heritage. He would also dedicate it to the many young people, now adults, and to their children, who came under the sway of his teachings and personality, and not least to his wife, Hannah, who was by his side in all his endeavors.

Herbert Haufrecht
Shady, New York

INTRODUCTION

This is the story of Mike Todd, largely as he told it himself. It forms a true folk biography or, more exactly, an autobiography. During the years since Mike Todd recorded his story, I have supplemented his recollections with testimony from people who knew him at various stages of his life. I have also arranged the material in more logical and chronological sequence. Yet, Mike Todd's story is essentially here in his own words.

How the recording came about forms a story in itself. To begin that story requires telling about Camp Woodland. For it was there that Mike's importance as a remarkable, yet "ordinary," individual was first fully recognized, and it was Mike's response to Camp Woodland's purpose and outlook that induced him first to mull over and then to record his reminiscences.

Camp Woodland was a summer camp for children, located at the head of Woodland Valley, near Phoenicia, New York in the heart of the Catskill Mountain Region. The camp functioned, under my direction from 1939 to 1962. Set up as a non-profit educational institution, the camp's program was infused with the fresh and vigorous ideas then being generated by the philosophy of progressive education.

The camp children really learned by doing. They built walks and bridges, remodeled bunks, and even constructed a stone amphitheater from material in an abandoned quarry. They learned to use their summer environment by growing vegetables in the rocky soil. They set up their own weather station, wove mats from local reeds, made pottery from red clay found in the vicinity, and developed a program of hiking and living outdoors.

But chiefly the campers learned from people, from their human environment. They met and interviewed their neighbors and visited the historical sites in the area. They danced the square dances taught them by George Van Kleeck, a local farmer and blacksmith who was also a dance caller. They helped collect the folk songs of the region, and sang them as they were taught by the local singers. They learned much about pioneer days when people had been knit together in close community, when they had worked together and played together.

This delving firsthand into the local history, the folklore and the folklife of the Catskill Mountain Region soon grew into a unique feature of Camp Woodland's program. Its educational goal sparked an ongoing search for the songs, the stories and the traditions clinging to the hills and valleys of this particular region that bespoke the manner of living of its people. Camp Woodland's focus was not just on discovery but on the saving and the use of the material. Local lore was to season the experience of children growing up in a country that has been notoriously profligate with its historical heritage.

So it was that over the years at Camp Woodland, the values of an almost bygone regional culture, so vividly represented by striking individuals like Mike Todd, contributed in an important way to the maturing of some hundreds of young city children, and they have never forgotten its influence.

Camp Woodland's emphasis on democracy, ecology, and a search for cultural roots within folk traditions anticipated by a quarter of a century the popular causes of the 1960s and 1970s. The camp was interracial, at a time when most Americans were being taught that interracial living was positively subversive.

The process of educating children to the culture and the resources of their summer environment began with field trips, which were geared to their age ranges, for groups from 6 to 16. We took many such expeditions throughout the Catskills from the more populous towns of the Hudson Valley westward to the smaller places along the upper reaches of the East and West Branches of the Delaware. Everywhere we sought indications of the way of life today, as well as tales out of the less accessible past.

But from its outset, the task of recovering much of the forgotten lore and local history of the Catskill Mountains was undertaken, not solely for the sake of Camp Woodland's children, but also for the benefit of the people of the region. That aspect of the project was more important because many of the more recent generation of Catskill people seemed to have lost touch with their own roots. Meanwhile, out of the trips, and out of return visits of many neighbors to Camp Woodland, we accumulated stories, square dance calls, ballads and songs, and invaluable knowledge of the way things used to be. Samples of material culture were also gathered, especially a variety of old work implements, from a logger's peavey to a husking peg to a dog treadmill.

Each August Camp Woodland sponsored the Folk Festival of the Catskill Mountains for the oral aspects of the local lore: the talk and the music, the dance, the plays based on regional history, and other imaginative celebrations allowing all present to enter into the sense of community. To it came the people we had met on our trips, and here they told and performed whatever they knew, while the campers and camp staff members participated by presenting what they had learned and absorbed from regional lore. Much that was obtained this way, as well as the records of trips, has been filed, classified and catalogued for further study. Since 1948, much of it has been preserved on tape, while some of the lore, particularly the ballads, songs and instrumental music, has been published in articles, in books and on recordings, beginning with Camp Woodland's own annual *Neighbors*.

But a further necessary project was the preservation and demonstration of the material culture of the region. Many of the older people we met on trips donated tools and useful things from the past. They also went among their neighbors and persuaded them to contribute. In a few years the collection of workaday items came to need storage space, a crew of camper-curators, and some on-the-spot instruction for the care and use of often obsolete implements of strange appearance and with even stranger names.

Then began a bolder dream, that of building a real Catskill folk museum on camp property. Construction of the museum became a project that involved all campers. The very process of its building was to teach youngsters and awaken their sense of identification with its contents and the way of life it embodied. Even before its completion, the museum would provide the Catskill community and its visitors with an idea of how things used to be. But by that time we had naturally thought of inviting Mike Todd to be our advisor on anything to do with old work ways.

Often the exploration of folklife has led to important and exciting discoveries quite by chance. Once several Camp Woodland counselors hitched a ride with a man from Margaretville, not far from Mike Todd's home in Dry Brook. When they told their driver they were from Woodland, whose undertakings were by then widely known and respected in the area, he suggested that Camp people ought to look up Mike Todd, that they would find him a man worth knowing. At that time Mike had recently retired as fire observer on Balsam Mountain.[1] His reputation as a bear hunter had reached us at camp several years before.

Following that chance meeting, the unnamed driver sent us a copy of an article about Mike in *Outdoor Life*[2]. I read the article, and set it aside temporarily. For just then, Camp Woodland was involved with several other interesting men and women of the Catskills, who were being brought to camp to share their music and their stories. There wasn't time to follow up another lead. But the advice was not forgotten, and like a seed it germinated at the right time.

By 1951 we were particularly interested in finding a locally knowledgeable person to serve as advisor to the planned museum of work implements. That

---

[1] The Balsam Mountain referred to in this book is Balsam Lake Mountain, elevation 3,720 ft.
[2] "Mike Todd, Bear Hunter" by Reuben R. Cross, 4/1940.

summer a group of Woodland campers with their counselor went up to Dry Brook. Mike Todd was living on the mountain road leading from there over to Millbrook Valley. From the first, Mike was very hospitable to our little group. Impressed with the stories and the manner of this wiry little man, the campers invited Mike Todd to visit Camp Woodland the next summer, and he agreed to come. Early in the summer of 1952 Mike first visited Camp Woodland. He came when we had another local visitor, Will Van De Mark, who came from a pioneer family in the Lackawack area. Will did not know Mike, but he had heard of him. The two old men hit it off very well together that weekend. We are fortunate to have a tape recording and a photograph as a remembrance of their fascinating exchange.

That year Mike first participated in the folk festival. He told some stories, and he also demonstrated how drivers of the old-time stage coaches cracked their long whips. That came up because another Catskill neighbor, Elwyn Davis, had just donated one to the museum. He meant for it to illustrate his singing of "The Stagecoach Driver's Lad." That was a ditty very popular about 1870, whose refrain begins: "Snap! crack! goes my whip, I whistle and I sing."

Every summer, from 1953 until his death in the spring of 1959, Mike came to Camp Woodland. He was deeply involved in our project. His was a many-sided personality, and his memory contained a veritable encyclopedia of Catskill folklore. All through those years he seemed to develop a deep consciousness of his mission to re-open the door to the past.

INTRODUCTION

At the end of Mike's last summer at Camp Woodland, in 1958, after the annual farewell banquet, and after the campers had gone home, he sat down with me, and for two days he recorded what he remembered of his life. Between us there was an understanding, never expressed in so many words, that this might be his last summer, that he might winterkill.

We stayed at it until he had told what he had to say. His story did not emerge in careful chronological order, and occasionally I interrupted him to ask questions or to prompt a reminiscence. This is the way his story came out. Although I later obtained some other details from neighbors and friends who had known Mike, and although I have had to reshuffle some of the sequence to round out the events, I have kept my editing to a minimum, the better to let Mike speak for himself.

Norman Studer
New York City

Folk Museum at Camp Woodland

Mike Todd in 1953
Collection of Eve Fairbairn Budd

1.

EARLY YEARS

Mike's story, as he related it to me, begins with his earliest ancestors:

The first Todd was Samuel—Samuel Todd lived to be 101 years old. He was buried over here at Clovesville and he dates back five generations, I guess, from me. At any rate, he had twelve sons. They all raised families, and that started a lot of Todds in Dry Brook. Samuel Todd, the father of all Todds, was a soldier under George Washington in the Revolutionary War. He came from England, I guess, and there was another one that came with him and settled in Connecticut, a brother. My grandfather was Dyer Todd, his father, Burr Todd.

The Samuel Todd Mike refers to was his great-great-grandfather. Samuel's son, Burr Todd, was his great-grandfather, as he says, and his grandfather was Dyer Todd. His father's full name was Hiram Burr Todd. On his mother's side were Joseph Haynes, his great-great-great-grandfather; Judson Haynes, his great-great-grandfather; Grant Haynes, his great-grandfather; Charlotte Haynes Genunge, his grandmother; and Elizabeth Genunge, his mother. Mike's given name was Merwin, also a family name on his mother's side. This information was relayed to me by Johnny Asher, who in turn received it from Jean Haynes Finch, a geneologist.

The first thing I ever remember is my grandfather carrying me on his back to Aunt Nancy Seager's. She was his sister, and on the way he had a big umbrel'. A little over a mile on the way there came up a shower. Well, I can remember hearin' the rain a-rattlin' on that big umbrel'. And that was in the early summer — I'd be 3 years old in September. That was my first remembrance of anything. That I can remember distinctly — hearin' the rain pour on top of that umbrel'.

Well, after that I was goin' up to the same place with my mother along towards fall. It was fall, beechnut time, and there was a drove of pigs come out of the woods, and they scairt me about to death, and I run and squealed and yelled, and she chased me up and cuffed my ears for runnin' away when she told me to stop.

We lived on what we called the Clark farm. There's a story goes in there. My father, when he was 21, he inherited from his mother's father fifteen hundred dollars. Dad let his father, Dyer Todd, hold the money for a farm he bought there. Then father's mother died, and Dyer Todd remarried. This second wife was quite keen and educated — a school teacher — and she was sharp. Father neglected gettin' any papers made up — and he couldn't prove he let his father have a penny. His father died — caught cold or something — and she trimmed my father out of every penny he had. Well, this Clark farm was loose, and grandfather hired it for pasture, one thing or another, and cut some of the medder over. It was a nice little farm but had no buildings on it, so my father went on it, and he got out some timber. Uncle Murph Seager started and helped him build a house and barn on the Clark property. Father bought it from Jim Clark, paid a thousand dollars for it and gave him a hundred down and paid him a hundred and twenty-five on contract. Jim Clark didn't own the place, and that made another mess.

Well, my father moved there, and I can remember walkin' behind the buggy wagon and my father leadin' me. My sister was born then, and my mother was in the wagon when we moved to the Clark place from the little white house on the Dyer Todd place. I can remember that. But I don't remember how old I was. That was about when I was 4 years old. My sister's name was Lottie—Charlotte. My brother's name was Gerald.

My father and mother treated me awful good, but they was a little rigid. You had to mind some. If they told you to do it, that was it. There was no guesswork about it. When I was a young guy, we were there on the Clark place and my father was drawin' manure on the hill on a piece of buckwheat. I was 5 or 6 years old. Anyhow, he had one ox that kicked to beat the band, a big ox. Something was the matter. The chains swung out on the nigh side—left hand side—of the team. My father went in beside him to fix the chain and I slipped on the other side with a mullein stalk, long mullein, and tickled the ox under the belly. He kicked and hit my dad on the knee and might have broke his leg. Well, to make it good, I ran. He hollered,"You come back here," and he grabbed his whip, a good un. I run the harder. When he hollered at me, he ketched me, and about the time he got me, he hit me on the point of the shoulder down to my hip. He streaked my back till the blood run out. Wasn't my mother mad! She told him a story. She said hittin' a kid as hard as he did wasn't no good at all. But I didn't tickle the ox again.

Our house was built of just plain hemlock boards, and sealed inside with hemlock, shingled with home-made shingles and sided on the outside—just boarded up and down and battened. Inside, the lower floor was two bedrooms and a living room. Upstairs was all one room. I slept alone there. It was pretty chilly gettin' up in the mornings, but I made it.

We raised flax on the Clark place, and I learned the trade from A to Z. My great-grandmother used to spin a lot of flax in our house. She was a short, thickset woman, and she was old; but she walked a great many miles in that Clark house spinning yarn and settin' by the flax wheel spinning flax. Her name was Betsy Haynes. The farm where she had lived belongs to the State now and is all overgrown with brush, over in Millbrook.

We had twelve to sixteen sheep, two black ones, nice big ewes, and the rest white. They'd take these ewes—the two black ones, and two whites—wash the sheep first in the crick, and they'd let 'em dry and shear 'em, and then they was washed agin and then bleached on the grass. Mixed together they'd make a nice grey wool. It would pick up fine. I've picked wool till I was so sick of it I didn't know what to do. Us kids at night would have to pick wool—pick it up loose; git it ready for the cardin' mill. I've seen father card wool with the hand card too. He'd make a nice wool, and I could do that myself, some.

When I was young, clothes was pretty much homemade. They used cloth for pants and shirts for youngsters called linsey-woolsey. They raised flax and spun it into a coarse thread and used it for warp — awful stout when it was twisted up tight — and they filled it in the loom with a woof of wool that had been beat up tight, and that made an awful good cloth.

John Haynes, a distant cousin of Mike's, recalled one of the comical effects of homespun that Mike observed during his school day:

Mike used to tell a story about Frank Fairbairn with homespun trousers and no underwear in the wintertime. Once Frank fell into the water and got the seat of his pants wet, and he then stands up to the wood fire to get dry. When he was called to the recitation bench by his teacher, he forgot that his pants were hot, and when he sat down, he told the other boys it was like sittin' in a pan of hot water. Mike would describe how he hollered.

I went to school some, went till I was 14 years old. We had two teachers that boarded around. My first teacher was a girl from Fleischmanns. I remember her well.

Robert Fairbairn, a second cousin, remembers him as a school mate:

He was a good scholar. I went to school with him, yes sir. In this little red schoolhouse down there, you betcha. He was always the leader. He always wanted to line up a bunch of kids, play horse. His long suit was to get a long blackberry vine. If one stepped out of line, he'd get you in. He used the vine for a whip.

In the year of '88, Uncle Murph Seager was taken sick with pneumonia, and the doctor brought him to; but my mother and Betsy Brunson, a neighbor woman, they helped take care of him, and they both got it, and they both died—one a day after the other—one on the 11th of December, 1888; the other, the 12th.

After my mother died, father and I lived on the Clark farm the best part of three years, and he worked out. He had a woman there, an old woman. Lottie and Gerald went up to Aunt Ida's, [Ida Todd's] I was the only one at home. I was just 11 when my mother died.

The effect of Mike's mother's death is vividly described by Mary Bogardus, whose ancestors grew up in Dry Brook Valley:

I think you will be interested in hearing the comment of an uncle of mine, who was born in Dry Brook and remembers Mike Todd as a small boy about eight years older than my uncle. He remembers him coming to school infrequently, a very lonely, raggedy and patched little fellow, struggling to learn his ABC's with no help from his relatives with whom his father had left him when he wandered away after his mother's death. He was pushed from pillar to post and my uncle says he had such "sad eyes" even as a young boy. In those days he was known as Mernie and usually carried with him, even at school, his old squirrel gun.

That Mike was often left essentially on his own after his mother died is corroborated by John Haynes, who said that Mike's father tried to evade responsibility for supporting his children after losing his wife. Mike, however, never mentioned this.

When I got to be 17 years old—I'd be 17 in the fall—we got a little farm up at the head of Dry

Brook, pretty near the last place up. Father and I moved there. We lived there two years, him and I. After a while he left and went to Chenango County, and I stayed alone two years after that.

Part of our house was of logs, part of it built of timber. We used the log part to live in. That was smaller and didn't take too much fuel to keep it warm. The other part was quite a big addition, and that we used as a hoop shop and a shingle shop. We made a lot of shingles. We made the hoops in winter. We both did the cookin' some. My dad was a pretty fair cook, and I got to be after a while.

I learned to make shingles at an early age. I split shingles before I was old enough to shave 'em. I split shingles before my mother died (along when I was 10, 11 years old). I liked to do that for a while; then it got monotonous. Father'd start the block, split the blocks out of the main block after he'd sawed the logs, get 'em all ready so there wasn't much trouble. The main thing was to mark 'em, mark 'em even.

We had a slab shanty built outside with a big fireplace to burn shavin'. There was an awful lot of shavin's with hoop makin' and shingle shavin'. The slab shanty was built with hemlock slabs, cut off peeled logs—good slabs. You just flattened one end and nailed it on the sill, slab inside, flat side outside. Then you took another slab and put it over the crack for a batten, makin' a double wall. The roof was made out of top shingles, a cheap job. You laid a fireplace out of stone, and used blue clay for mortar. Make it big and high so you could throw in an armful of shavin's. It had a ground floor back— about half way back—so you could set nothin' on fire. The building was about 26 feet long, 15 feet wide, not too high, peaked roof.

What my father liked to work best was layin' stone. He'd lay a nice wall. He'd lay the straightest wall without a line I ever seen, and he done a lot of field walls, and he had a patent on layin' a fireplace, and he never failed on havin' one that would draw when he got through with it. I learned to lay stones right with father. I learned the hull cheese from him. Well, it was kinda natural for me. I was a little ingenious and I ketched on fast. We's got along pretty good together, we laid some cellars, and foundations, and worked on some highways, on culverts and arched bridges.

Father trained steers. He was always makin' pets of 'em so they wasn't afraid of him, not a bit. He broke horses, too, and colts. He said you had to have a lot of patience. He did have a lot of patience — 'lowed if you wanted to train an animal you mustn't hurt 'em. He pushed and pulled and tried not to learn 'em too much at once, and to learn a little so they know what he was talkin' about. When he got 'em broke thoroughly at about 2 years old, they would do anything he told 'em to. If they didn't — when he was sure they knowed what he was talking about — if they wanted to be mischievous and a little bit mean, then he'd whip 'em, make 'em mind. But they had to know first — and he had to know that they did know.

He doctored animals — afore they was any veterinarians. I learned a lot from him. I had a book that I'd study, a dictionary to find out some of the words.

I remember a tannery at Margaretville. The man's name was George Messenger. It was just up the Roxbury road where the bridge is. He used to tan leather on the half. Father used to get a side of sole leather — half a side, or something like that. It took a year and a half to tan. Father used to get that leather and he was a pretty good shoemaker, and he'd get that leather to make boots. The first pair of shoes I ever had he made out of high bootleg leather tops. I didn't learn that business much — 'course I could tap a sole and so on, but I never tried to make a shoe.

I learned to work steel, to make cast steel and make a chisel of it. They used to use ['em] on flagstones, hand drills — bore holes in stones to make 'em come apart, plug-and-feather they called it. I used to go to town with my father on a load of shingles; and while the team was eatin' and restin' and he was gettin' the load unloaded, I'd go down to the blacksmith shop. I'd watch the old blacksmith work, make different things, and lots of times I'd get some crackers and cheese. He'd have a lot of tools to be sharpened from the quarries there. And I'd watch him sharpen and temper them, while I ate my lunch. That's the way I learned to temper steel. I learned to heat it and work it. Later I worked with a feller in the quarry. He was a good tool sharpener, and I learned from him. I quarried in Dry Brook. There was a quarry on the old Clark place.

Both Robert Fairbairn and John Haynes remembered his skill at the forge. Said Robert:

As far as steel goes, he'd temper you a piece of steel the way you wanted it. He knew the colors. Learned how to temper, and I think learned by himself, elst by practice. Because he never was a blacksmith, never worked in a blacksmith shop.

Said John:

Mike would do some work in the shop, or build something, and he would say, "It ain't very pretty for nice, but it's hell for stout."

I learned about butcherin' by goin' with my father and helpin' him. He was a good hand. We used to go 'round. We had a big pan to heat water, and a tub and went with a horse and rig, go 'round Dry Brook and butcher pigs. Once in a while butcher beef. We got 50 cents apiece for hogs.

When they had a good beech crop, they'd take a drove of pig shoats and turn 'em loose in the woods. Farmers'd get together and they'd cut 'em in the ear — a little notch or something, and they'd build a pen out of logs, jest a cover, and put a lot of leaves in for a nest. So the pigs would go in, and they'd make a trough and give a little corn once in a while and a little salt — had to salt 'em so they'd stay. They'd work right in the beech nuts and get fat, awful good.

Billy DeSilva and Howard bought a lot of shoats and put 'em in the woods over in Millbrook, and they had two gangs, they was sixty-six in the two flocks of pigs they had. And they weighed a hundred pounds apiece when they put 'em in the beech nuts; and when they took 'em out to kill, some of 'em would weight a hundred and seventy.

I butchered 'em. Had some help because they'd go in the woods, and I had a .22 rifle, a Stevens' Crack Shot, and shot 'em in the head. They'd knock 'em down and stick 'em in the belly and we'd kill four, take 'em over. We had a fire under a big kettle, and we'd throw some water in the barrel and scald 'em, dress 'em and go back and get another load. The last five or six of 'em got wild and it took quite a little huntin' to git a shot at one and git close enough. But we got 'em butchered after a while and all sold. I worked, I think, four days, and got a dollar a day and board. We killed fifteen or sixteen a day—four of us—four good active fellers. We was fast at the scrapers. I knowed how to temper the water to scald 'em. There was one time I could dress a pig that weighed 200 pounds in two minutes and a half.

I done a lot of surveyin', that is, helped. I done a lot of chainin'. I chained one of the lines from the side of Eagle Mountain down across the head of Burnham Holler, and we went right on though. I kept a book on that—kept it all the way through. I was on the head of the chain and I kept a book and turned it in every night: the distance to the gullies, the depth of the gullies, go down in and up out of it—surface measure—that's the way they used to measure the ground. And we followed that line out of the valley. And we went over the mountain— over the edge of Hangbird's Nest, big boardin' house—you know, that is back of the old Slide Mountain House, up pert' near to the head of Big Indian Valley. Dave Hilton, the ranger at Phoenicia and I measured that, and that house was a monument, and we hit that on center. Was 7 links short, a link in a surveyor's chain is 7 inches and 2 millimeters. Well, we run that line from there, right on the top of Little Hemlock Mountain, to Winnisook Lake, across Winnisook Lake and right through the head to the East Branch of the Neversink and over the wing of that plateau that's on Peekamoose Range to a monument on the head of Watson Holler, and we was only 8 links short of measurement when we got to that monument. They's about

600 chains distance—80 chains a mile, right through the wilderness.

Uncle Murph Seager was a great woodsman and quite a scholar, a homemade scholar because he studied all the while. A great mechanic, a good blacksmith and carpenter—learned all hisself. Uncle Murph was a great mathematician. There was a feller named Decker, he had a contest once with hard examples. They'd have those contests in a home and give each other problems. Well somebody gave Decker a problem he couldn't solve, so he brought it to Uncle Murph. Murph worked it out in algebra and Decker didn't know nothin' about it. He learned me a lot of tricks about woodcraft, fishin' and travelin' through the woods. One time when this map was being made, I was a kid about 13 or 14 years old, and a feller came to Margaretville and hired a feller there as a guide. His name was Will Anderson, a young lad. He didn't know the country, was no account. They was a-goin' up Spruce Mountain to put up a flag, one due east or west—whatever it was—going to put it up a tree. They got lost and laid in the woods all night. They didn't know how to get out—they didn't know nothin' about the woods anyway.

Well, they got out of Dry Brook after a while, and they come out at Uncle Murph's, and I was thar. The fellow was about bushed, and he laid over for a day or two. Then he wanted to go up Graham Mountain and put up a flag there, and he asked Uncle Murph if he could get a guide, and Murph says, "Yes, I'll get you a guide."

I'd been up there a hundred and one times, pert' near, with Uncle Murph, and they had a good trail from the old Tappan Road. Well, when he got ready to start, I come around. I was goin' with him.

The feller says, "No, I don't want no kid as a guide."

Uncle Murph said, "Never mind the kid—he'll take you up thar."

We went up and we got the flag pole fastened to a tree. He says put the white flag where they could see from one point to the other. There was beginnin' to growl and grunt a thundershower, I told him we'd better slip right off here in the holler. "We can get there in an hour this way—a short cut. The way we came up is roundabout."

"No, no," he says, "I wouldn't go down there. It's awful steep—too rough."

So we went down the mountain his way. About halfway down the mountain there came a rain—couldn't see or hear nothing. It thundered and lightnin'ed and we crawled under a rock. I saw an overhang, and he got just as wet as a mop, and so did I before we got out. I laughed at that.

The landlords had a land grant of big territory here. It was called the Hardenburgh Patent. A man by the name of Tappan, surveyor, ran a road from Kingston, from the Hudson River to the Delaware. When the Tappan Road was completed, it ran up Dry Brook. They built a forge and drawed in iron so that the settlers would come in and take up the land. They got quite a territory settled in that way.

Mike's appraisal of the way Dry Brook was opened for settlement is borne out by a letter written by Mike's own father to his niece, Miss Bessie Kittle in Kingston. The letter, in the possession of Edwin Hunt Kittle was made available to me by Mrs. Lena Knapp Haynes of Dry Brook:

Dear Niece:

I read your letter and was glad as well as surprised to get a letter from you. We are all well at present for wonder. . . You spoke of giving you a little history of the Old Forge. Well, here it goes as Grandpa Seager has told me. The foundry building was built in the year 1812 in wartime with England by a Stock Company and Grandfather Merwin was one of them, I will give you the names of some that I remember, Samuel Merwin, Joseph Haynes, Benjamin Milks, Gideon Cramm, Squire Hunt, Henry Brown, William Whalen & C.

Now then the fool part of it was they hawled all the iron ore from West Point down the Hudson River with Oxen and Carts and some Horses, they run a flourishing business making iron until the summer of 1815. The war with England had closed in 1814, the price of iron went down, and they could not afford to make it the expense of hawling iron ore so far and the iron they made to market so theyer sope buble busted and the old forge died a natural death.

There was two reasons why they came to Dry Brook to make iron: the old landlord Cunningham owned all the land far and near and started this iron foundry in order to help sell his land, and wood was plenty and have it for the cutting. In making iron they have to use charcoal burned from wood and ore.

Your Pa will tell you how coal pits are burned. . . One thing more I will write—it may not help you any—is this. Grandfather Merwin was the carpenter that framed the old forge building. I got the square he used, he made it himself as he was a blacksmith. Also the square has his name on it—date 1803, I have the old relic now. Anyone wishing to see it can call at my office,

Lovingly your uncle
[signed] H. Burr Todd

The landlords charged so much rent, and the tenants couldn't pay it. They'd take the stock away from the tenants as pay. That got the mob mad. A man by the name of Steele was Undersheriff, and he was going to have a sale up the Tremperskill near Andes. He came there to sell the stock, but the [tenants disguised as] Indians came from everywhere to prevent him. Warren Scudder, the High Chief of the Down-Renters, 'lowed Steele would be permitted to go ahead with his sale, but they would never drive any cattle off the place. Steele jumped his horse over the fence and Scudder jumped in after him with a double-barreled blunderbuss. Warren hollered for the Indians to shoot, and stopped Steele dead with his horse there and then. The mob scattered hither and yon.

Uncle Murph Seager knew all about it, as did other old people. Uncle Murph told me all about it. George C. Murphy was one of those old landlords. He had a big territory of land, and he sold it to George Gould. Last six years he took the lumber off it. I went around with Uncle Murph to see that no poachers were taking the lumber. That was way back when I was a kid, 10 or 12 years old. He didn't take no part in the Anti-Rent Wars, but he knew all about it and see some of it.

I can remember as a young school kid finding in the vicinity of the Old Forge chunks of fused iron ore; can also remember seeing traces of the old road which the old-timers said was the one used by the ox teams to haul the iron ore. The road [went] over the mountain at Highmount, then over another ridge down into the Seager Valley.

The long struggle between tenants and landlords, which became known as the Anti-Rent War, touched Dry Brook Valley, as it did almost every community in the Catskills. Besides the stories told by Mike Todd, we gathered other tales that related to this exciting and significant episode in American history. Mrs. Lena Haynes invited several elder women to come to her house to talk about the old days. I taped the interview, and this story was told about the Anti-Rent War, by Nora Baker:

> I have been so disgusted with myself to think that I didn't ask my grandfather, Will Graham, more about the Anti-Rent War. He owned a farm way up on the mountain—he wasn't a tenant—but he was present on the Earle farm when Steele was shot. He was right there...
>
> My uncle went out west when the trouble came and Steele was killed. I know Grandfather Graham told about it. My uncle was out in the woods when he heard the sheriff's posse talking. They were after him. He was on the brink of a ledge, so he said, "I went and grabbed a big rock—all I could hold. I rolled it over the edge." Then he said, "I run and hid in the brush." He said, "They come and looked over the ledge, and they said, 'Well, if he went over there, he's dead anyway. No more use looking for him.' I kept quiet. They walked away, and I was safe."

John Haynes adds another dimension to the Anti-Rent conflict in Dry Brook Valley:

On top of the road that comes from Fleischmanns to Rider Hollow there's a big rock. And at present there's a post in that rock with a sign on it pointing the way to the Belleayre Ski Slope. That hole was originally put there to put up an old flag—Anti-Rent flag, Anti-Rent War. A man by the name of John Todd told me that. And he said it was full of nails and their heads filed off so that no one could climb the pole to steal the flag. It was made out of muslin and valuable in those days. But later somebody cut the pole down and took the flag away. No one knows who got the Anti-Rent flag. Probably made into a petticoat.

2.

BORN A HUNTER

I was born with an interest in huntin', I guess. I remember when I was a kid, the first bear I see my Uncle Frank killed. He hung it up in the old sawmill. Well, I was a little feller, and I went up there, and I seen the bear, and I looked him over for half an hour.

Just as quick as I got old enough to carry a gun at all, I got a little shotgun, and I'd go up on Balsam Mountain to gather balsam gum from blisters on trees. I'd take the gun along with me. The gum would run just like thick syrup in hot weather. I took a hatchet and a short-handled axe and nails, and I'd make me a wagon and run it up on the mountain, and I gathered it—got a dollar a pint—made a funnel, had a bottle and squeezed the blister so the stuff would run into the bottle. I was goin' up there, and I got pert' near the top. The dog was with me—a shepherd dog, and he came down the hill a yellin' murder. I heard him bark, and then I heard him scream, and he picked up a bear—an old bear—and the animal walloped him and then chased him. The bear came right down the hill after him, and I had the little shotgun loaded with fine shot. I shot and missed him, but he turned around anyway. I didn't hit him in the face. I don't think I hit him over the top of the head, in the back if I hit him at all. He turned around and went back up the hill. I had only one shot and that's the first bear I seen in the woods and the first one I ever shot at.

Mike's affinity for guns and hunting is legendacy; and as Mike said himself, it started at a precocious age. John Haynes recalled:

Mike always had a gun over his left arm. I could tell a story that brings out how handy he was with a gun. I and Mike sat down on a high point on the rocks. We'd been hunting kingfishers, and I reached for my gun and Mike for his. And Mike shoots the kingfisher while I was trying to find out what's the matter with the gun, because I had the wrong gun. It didn't bother Mike. He shot the kingfisher all right. He lived with a gun in his hand, practically.

Bear huntin' was my choice. I was always crazy to hunt bear, and I didn't know why. My father never was. I didn't see no danger, and I couldn't get anyone to go with me, so I hunted a lot alone. Stayed in the woods a lot at night alone when it wasn't too cold weather.

The first bear I killed was with a Springfield army musket. Bought it off Charley Dick at Margaretville while I and my father lived up thar in the woods. He had a Winchester rifle and he wouldn't let me have it, so I had a little money and I bought the Springfield. It was a long, heavy, bungling gun barrel, was 36 inches long and weighed 9 pounds — think .68 calibre. He had some of the cartridges they used in the Civil War made out of paper. You tear off the end of 'em and ram the paper right down, bullet and all, with a steel ramrod. Well, they kicked sumpin' scandalous, and the gun it pulled awful hard. I took the lock off—father, he helped me. I filed the ketch so it didn't pull so hard. That first bear I killed was when I was 16 years old, and Frank Fairbairn was with me. He was a year older. And we started out huntin' and found this bear track and had the luck to follow him into a ledge in about four hours.

Frank had a single-barreled, muzzle-loaded gun, and I had a single-barrel gun, muzzle-loaded, and the bear started to come out of the hole, and Frank shot first through his nose, and then he went back in the hole, jumped right backwards. Then he started to come out again, and I shot and hit him in the left eye, back in his brain, and killed him instantly.

We had to get a snare on his neck to pull him out. Had quite a job to get him out—and dragged him—wasn't a little ways from where I lived—about 2 miles. As a couple of young hunters, we were pretty proud of ourselves.

The first thing I killed with my first gun to amount to anything, I came pert' near bein' licked. I was 18 years old. I went up alongside Gould's park fence one day alone, all by myself. Elmer Gavette went along the fence every day. Once in a while he'd have a fit, and he'd be sick for a week, and he'd call on me to go around the fence. We'd be hired to go around and see that a tree hadn't fallen across. Two-thirds of the way was through the forest. It was a deer and elk park. They had a lot of elk in that and some young uns. I went along as far as Judson's Ridge; and they was a drove of elk up there, I picked out a young un. He was as big as a good sized deer, and I shot him with that rifle, that Springfield rifle.

As he related to Johnny Asher many years later, "When I had him in the sights, I could taste him."

There was a place where the fence went over the ledge about 2 foot high, and they laid a stone that run up to the wire fur mebber 5 or 6 feet to make it so's little things couldn't git through. I took the stones out very carefully, and I dragged the thing through. I picked up every leaf that had a drop of blood on it, and I dragged it off down into the timber holler a ways and dressed it — took its innards out and laid the stone back nice as a pin. Looked everything over and there was no blood nowhar. I either turned every leaf that had a drop of blood on it, picked it up and put it under a stone or sumpin', very careful to blot out my tracks. Then I took the thing down to the Turner Holler Brook and took the hide off and cut it in two, and then I could carry half of it and the hide up to a little point in the hemlocks and hide it. Went back and got the other half and put that with it. I went home and when it got dark hitched up my horse and buckboard, and I set a box on the back of the buckboard, a dry goods box, and I set my meat on that. Next day I hid the hide, and then I went and buried it.

Well, my father scowled a little, but he didn't say nothin'. We ate the meat up. It took us quite a while. And when we had the last on the table he told me, "I'm goin' to tell you somethin'. If you take any more elk, I'm goin' to kick your behind." I knew that's what would happen, and I didn't kill any more.

Mike was a dead shot. According to John Asher, Will Ackerley, another friend of Mike's, would tell how Mike hit a hedgehog up in a tree. It was a mighty blow and "that there hedgehog trapezed."

There was one time when I can remember when I was young when there were no deer in our section. I was a young lad. There was one old stand of deer that lived in the swamps of the Willowemoc. There were no game laws. That's why there were few deer. Jim Decker followed one from the Willowemoc to the head of Dry Brook right at the old sawmill up there. I was 9 or 10 years old then. He run that deer all over Dry Brook 'fore he ketched him. When he ketched him, he was killed.

When the game laws first came in, when the first game protector came in, he must have had a tough time. Well he mighta, he was quite a feller. If you had a dollar or two, or a pinta liquor, you got by with a lot of things. Ed Burhans, he was one of the first game catchers. There was twelve of them. It was way back, I don't know when, but I remember I seen that Ed Burhans.

3.

MUSIC EDUCATION

I first became interested in music very young. I played a jews harp as quick as I got my teeth. I played the harmonica when I was 9 years old. My father was a pretty good violinist. He played the guitar some. He never did try to teach me to play the violin, and I never did try.

Once when I was workin' over at Alder Lake, there was a colored feller there. He came from Kingston. His name was Combat—George Combat. He played the banjo, and it sounded good. I learned to play the banjo and sing some songs; and when we parted from the job, I could pick the banjo pretty fair, could play three or four tunes. I could sing two or three songs, but I never went to work or something and stopped. I neglected buyin' a banjo, and I forgot the whole thing.

There was a feller there—a foreman on the George Gould place by the name of Keator—and he couldn't get enough men to do the work in the neighborhood so he built a house and got twenty-five Italians to work. One of them was an accordion player, and I learned an Italian tune I played on the mouth organ. They was one of them played the bones with one hand, right handy. I took a notion to it and kept lookin' at him and after a while I rattled 'em a little. He gave me a set—made out of wood—hard maple. Well, I got so I could rattle 'em, and I rattled 'em with him so I got the time and learned a little of it myself. I was about 16 years old then.

Mike's musical ability, like his hunting prowess, was known throughout the area, as Robert Fairbairn maintained:

He was a professional mouth organ player. You take him on the mouth organ, Uncle Murph Seager on the violin, and Lou, my cousin, on the organ, and you was well-entertained. They played at home. I don't ever remember them playing at dances. He'd tell his stories everywhere, get into a bunch, then afterwards he'd laugh. All you had to do was give Mike a couple of hookers [i.e. drinks of liquor], and he was off.

Mike's long-time friend, Waldron Dumond, also witnessed a memorable concert:

A friend of mine came up with me when I taught school in the Catskills and thought he'd like to spend a weekend with me, and we came up. We decided we'd hear some old-time fiddling, so we bought two quarts of whiskey and set them up in the center of the floor, and Mike went to Arena and got an old man and his son who used to play fiddles. And Mike of course had the harmonica and bones, and they started playing; and as they played, the music increased in volume in inverse proportion to the line on the bottle. It was a rare evening, I can tell you. Those fiddlers were very good.

The curious thing about them, they would play and never crack a smile. Just as serious about it as though they were playing for the Boston Symphony.

4.

A STORY-TELLER'S EDUCATION

My great-grandmother told us kids some awful spook stories to make us afraid so we'd go to bed. My mother'd be away somewhere takin' care of somebody that was sick. Great-grandmother was about 90 when she died. I remember one of her stories about a man that had a rope line for a horse. He took the harness off and left it in the field, turned the horse loose, goin' to dinner, and when he came back the lines was all twisted up, so it took him a half day to get 'em all unraveled again. Witches done it. Couldn't get butter and they'd lay it to a witch, and they'd heat a horseshoe red hot and throw it into the churn and that would warm it enough to make the butter come, and they'd lay it to the witches. I used to go with Old Man Graham when he went up the holler fishin' just to git him to tell me a bear story.

It appears that the ability to tell a good story ran in Mike's family. Mike seemed drawn to anyone with that talent and was always ready to learn another story to add to his own repertoire. It took an excellent memory, an ear for detail, and a dramatic wit. According to Mike's fans, he had all those qualities in abundance. Said Waldron Dumond:

Mike told stories well. He never forgot anything. Some went way back to Uncle Murph Seager. He could tell you all about Uncle Murph and the old mill. Yes, he had a remarkable memory. He, like many of the Todds, was keen mentally. When they do go out, some of them have high places. Mike's uncle was head of the Normal School at Plattsburgh. Other Todds have gone out and have become quite famous. Mike had intelligence, but no book learning. He never read any books. It would't take much to get Mike started telling stories. Somebody told one that was interesting to Mike, and he would come right back with one that was just as good or sometimes better. He would always hold his audience when he was telling one of these stories because he was an excellent performer.

His friend, Cecil Polley, his relatives, Mary Liddle, Stratton Todd and Nate Haynes, also vouched for his reputation as an entertaining conversationalist. Cecil remembered how Mike used to entertain city men who came to the Catskills to fish and hunt. Listening to Mike was part of the vacation. If a camp where these men stayed was planning to have Mike over for an evening, all the other camps in the vicinity were notified. Mike was sure of a full house and the hunters were well-entertained. Some of the hunters were college men who said they had never heard such interesting stories. Mike's fame grew to the point where he went to New York City to hunters' expositions and told tall tales.

Mary Liddle recalled that when she was a young girl, the young people used to get up parties led by Waldron Dumond and hike up Balsam Mountain to the fire tower for a picnic. Invariably Mike, as the tower official, told some of his stories. Mike bragged about having a pet snake, but Mary never once saw the snake show up.

5.

LIFE OF A POACHER

After leavin' the house at the head of Dry Brook, I worked on a farm over at Rose's Brook once and hired out for another man two seasons. Then I went back to Dry Brook. That was the time I tried to get a job at Gould's [the George Gould Estate]. They wouldn't give my father a job — why, I never did know. They was my own blood cousins, too, second cousins. [George] Gould and my father was great friends. I always thought it was a matter of jealousy. He was afraid my father would get a better job than he wanted him to. Father needed a job because he had a family to take care of. He was a good stone layer. He couldn't get a job and I couldn't. Then I began to trespass and sell fish.

John Haynes verified that jobs were hard to come by:

>Times was pretty tough. There was a lot of men like Mike. They worked for their board. Wages at tops: a dollar and half a day. There was lumbering in those days. At that time there was five or six sawmills in Dry Brook. The Goulds hired a few men. That was the big employment in the valley. Mike'd worked for

'em. He also worked for the camps in Beaverkill. His job mostly was handling steel, sharpening drills. Alder Lake, for example, it was a camp built by the people that owned the Ulster and Delaware Railroad. They carried on a lot of work—road construction and so on. Mike worked there. His job was a handyman, the smith who sharpened the tools.
 He went from pillar to post. He worked here as long as he could. He stayed with Uncle Frank; then with his father. They'd try to batch it a bit. He was a very good worker if you could keep him at it. When he got paid he'd like his "cold tea." That was the worst thing about Mike. He liked his "cold tea."

Waldron Dumond explained the local attitude toward trespassing:

He did a lot of poaching. Well, he didn't poach any more'n the rest of us. In that day there was natural warfare between the game warden and the natives. We lived at the head of the hollow; and if we wanted to see some meat, we went out and got it. The game wardens didn't bother us too much 'cause they knew better. Mike told me once how he got Joe DeSilva. He was game protector in those days. Joe DeSilva was after him, and he said, "I got up on the side of a hill, and there was a spring, and I looked down and there was Joe DeSilva drinkin' right out of the spring. I took the old Winchester, and I just leveled her right out and hit about 2 feet right alongside of his face. Joe got out of there."
 There wasn't much work in Dry Brook. Well, not until George Gould came in, that would be

true. Mike [worked] as a bark peeler and also a man that got out lumber and so on, as did the other people. But after the Gould people came in, they hired everybody in the valley, practically everybody worked for Gould, and the farms more or less went to pot. He took a 200 foot strip along the streams, but they still had their farms and worked for him. When George Gould died they had to come back to farming, then some of 'em did have quite a time keeping alive.

After the big estates came in, the local person would come into conflict with the watchers. It was a tough proposition. You'd fish with one eye up and down the brook and one on your line. The local people did not take badly to the watchers. It was considered a day's work, and people didn't mind it. Some was more lenient than others. Some would arrest their own mother if they caught her at it. Others, of course, would be more lenient. It was a good job. Nothing to do but walk patrol day and night. Of course they were on duty all the while. That was their job, and they did a pretty good job.

Mike got the job of creek watcher for the Goulds in a unique way.

Money was scarce, and the Fleischmann's Yeast people built a lot of big houses over at Fleischmanns. They're fallin' down now. The places they used to have ridin' horses is all fallen in on the mountain road. Well, John Blish owned two farms there, and he was a big rugged feller and he was land poor, and he had hard work to pay anything, but he fell right in sellin' lots of them Fleischmann men and old Senator Fleischmann and the boys; and when he died seventy-odd years old, he was worth two hundred thousand dollars. I sold him a lot of game. I'm gettin' to the bottom of it—to tell what market I had—and he took all the trout I could catch. The partridges and rabbits—not too much rabbits—the partridges was worth 75 cents a pair. There wasn't much in the way of game laws at the time. 'Course they was game laws, but that was before the game protectors. Two years I stayed alone at the head of the valley I didn't do nothing but fish. I caught a lot of fish out of them back streams. I got 50 cents a pound for dressed trout with the heads on. I kept that up for two seasons and a half; and they knowed, they knowed very well—the Superintendant of the Gould's knowed—I was gettin' fish out of their lake. They knowed I was gettin' trout out of the crick, and they was only one way to stop it, was to hire me for crick watcher. That's how I got the job.

I didn't only trespass on the Goulds, but on Balsam Lake Club and on the Millbrook Club and over on the West Branch of the Neversink, on Old Man Cook and Ruff. I used to git trout there—a long way to go.

I never did get caught at it, but I come awful close to it. I could run pretty good, and I'd get away. I'd always fish at night, you know, I and George Green. Well, the way it was—there was three or four of us went over to Furlough Lake fishin' one night. One feller was very courageous. He had a club a couple of feet long, with a hole through it and a strap on his wrist. He was goin' to knock the watchman to death if he came near him. George Green and I didn't think that was the way of doin' things at all. So George says, "I'd rather get caught," he says, "than have a man killed." And he says, "We'll stay along the lower end when Charley comes here."

Charley Knapp, the crick watcher, was a scary feller—the same feller I told you about ran away from a bear one day. He was a blacksmith watchin' crick some at night.

We stayed around the lower end of the lake, and we had a place where we could hide awful easy, and we didn't get out on no log. We stayed on the shore, and was fishin' off there and catchin' trout. We were close to the park gate inside the park. We had a good place to run in the woods. The first thing we know we heard the gate squeak, and I whispered to George, I said, "They's somebody over there."

Frank Fairbairn—I wasn't going to mention his name, the poor bugger's dead now—he was the feller that was goin' to kill Charley Knapp, with a club, and he had it all ready. He was above us about 50 feet out on a log, a little ways, fishin', and Charley got along—well, right opposite us, and we sneaked right down behind the log, right down close. It was part moonlight, the fish was workin' good. We lay right down there. We wasn't going to let Frank pick onto him with that club at all—didn't intend to—much better go to jail than have a man killed. But when Frank discovered him, he was about 30 feet from the end of the log. He went off that log like a scairt cat. All the runnin' I ever see, he done and got away slick and clean and went up the lake and warned the other fellers.

I and George laid right still—never moved, stayed right quiet and didn't make no fuss at all. He had steady nerves, and I had some myself. Charley went right by, and he went around the lake, looked things over and then left for home. Then we went back to fishin' and finished our mess of fish, and then we went home and nobody got hurt.

And the man that was so courageous—was goin' to knock Charley Knapp down with a club and pummel him all up—I don't know how fur he run, but he lost his fish pole, 50 feet long good fish line, and I went back next day and found it.

John Haynes related another adventure they had with Charley Knapp:

Mike and several other men got poaching and full of hard cider and feeling pretty good, and they thought they'd throw the creek watcher, Charley Knapp, into the creek. So they sent a couple of men to wake him up. Made some noise. They came back down. All gathered around the rocks and talkin' about what they'd do. About that time Charley came down, show a few bullets through the tops of trees, and the men went in every direction—never did get together again.

Other poaching adventures were more risky:

Jim Decker was quite a character at Willowemoc. He was into a little bit of everything, run store and one thing and another—sold partridges other people snared. He'd buy hoops, anything you had to sell.

Beebe and Jack Smith and some of the other settlers snagged an awful lot of partridges for Decker. He furnished the wire he found in his barn under the floor—the snare wire. They put out the snare along with a little fence with a hole. Jim was out in Livingston Manor, and he was in a hotel, drinked a little, got too noisy, talked too much. George

Stewart, his brother-in-law, was tendin' bar, and he took down a little of that story and handed it to the constable.

Jim Decker was takin' partridges down to New York in two suitcases, and he had forty-seven of 'em all dressed, and Joe, the constable, captured him and fined him quite sharp. Jim didn't give the Smiths away. I'd been over in Willowemoc for a dog—he got away from the Gould place. I hadn't seem Jim Decker, and wouldn't have known him if I had seen him.

Jim knowed if he gave the Smiths away it'd be just too bad for him, so he 'lowed there was a feller by the name of Todd—had a black moustache—came over to Willowemoc, and a feller by the name of Constable, that sold him the partridges. That got me mad, and when Joe came after me, wanting me to go before the Justice of Peace, I said, "Captain, I hain't snared partridges, and if I had, I'd see you in Hell before I'd go with you."

Unseen by anyone, Mike came down out of the woods from deer hunting right next to where John Crook's bull was grazing. The bull came after him, and Mike decided to teach him a lesson by shooting right through his horns. Unfortunately, he miscalculated and killed the bull "dead as a mitt." Meanwhile, Claude Haynes, unaware of the shooting, passed through. He was also on his way home from a day of hunting and was immediately charged with shooting the bull. He could only deny it vehemently, but all the while he harbored secret suspicions. At least thirty years later the truth came out. Said Claude to Mike one day when, both retired, they were having a visit, "By the way, who killed John Crook's bull?" Mike threw back his head and laughed so hard the whole valley must have heard him.

6.

A FUGITIVE IN PENNSYLVANIA

After two years of living in the log house alone, I quit the cabin entirely. My father had got married again and was livin' in Chenango County on a farm. I still had a horse and some blankets. I had a good cookstove, and I kept it stored in a shop down at Uncle Frank's, and the blankets were there in the house. But I didn't use any of that stuff for quite a few years, and then I was workin' for Will Graham, sawin' in the spring. We had to saw all the lumber that we got out in the winter while the snow was goin' out of the woods, 'cause the water mill was up at the head of the valley, and there was quite a little watershed above it; but when the snow was gone and the pond wouldn't fill up, you couldn't saw very good. They had to saw nights. I sawed nights and Will sawed days, and we run the mill twenty-two hours out of twenty-four. We got the sawin' done. I sawed for 75 cents a day and board, ten hours a day. Then when I made him pay me a dollar a day, he was mad at me, and he didn't like it at all, and he had to pay it or I wouldn't work for him; I'd go to work for somebody else. Well, that made a little crossup between him and me. Then I went to borrowin' a bear trap from him. His grandfather gave him one—gave his brother Hiram one—they was great bear hunters. Old Man Hiram Graham bought those two bear traps weighing 42 pounds apiece. Grizzly bear traps. He got them from Montgomery Ward for about $8 apiece.

Well, I went to borrow one to set in the spring, after we got through loggin' it—to ketch a bear—a bear's fur is jest as good in the spring up to the 1st of May as it is any time—1st of June better. But he cursed me and wouldn't let me have it.

Frank Fairbairn worked in the mill. But he was in my crew at night, and he wasn't of age and I was, and him and I made up to borrow those traps when they wasn't anybody at home. I got Frank to help me, which was all wrong naturally. So we went and borrowed those traps one night when there was nobody at home and lugged them off and was going to set 'em.

They mistrusted me right away, and they questioned Frank. They knowed he was probably along with me because him and I was huntin' some together. Well, they pitched onto him, and he gave it away, so they got out a warrant. The Board met Saturday at Pine Hill, and they couldn't get a warrant in Millbrook because over there they wouldn't give 'em a warrant. Will Green and Hiram Todd and my father was good friends, and they wouldn't give him a warrant, said it didn't amount to anything anyway—they had their traps back.

Will Graham was still mad at me for makin' him pay a quarter more for workin' for him, and he was going to make me some trouble. I was boardin' at Old Man Christians', cutting logs for him. I'd been to town, bought me a pair of boots. When I came back, Old Man Christians told me, "They found out about you and this bear trap deal. Frank gave it away—told Will you and him was goin' to set the trap."

Well, the next day was Sunday, I was goin' home—down to Uncle Frank's to see my brother. I had a dollar and 22 cents. My brother had a dollar, he gave me that. Well, that night I met Uncle Rube Todd. He wasn't my uncle, but I always called him uncle. He was an old man—a big man. He didn't like the Grahams—they didn't hitch very good. He 'lowed if I let Grahams catch me, he'd kill me. I said, "Uncle, you needn't worry. I'm goin' to leave the country tonight."

So that night, at eight o'clock, I started for the Pennsylvania Line—66 miles afoot. I went up through the Gould lake—shortcuttin' it a little—down Millbrook and up the Cat's Ladder and up on Cross Mountain Road down to Turnwood. Right along by Will Walmsley's sap house there was a pair of horses out the back.

It was a bright crystal night—22nd of October, 1900. Well, I had a lot of rawhide string in my pocket, and I had a pair of woollen gray pants on. There was a pair of horses there, and one was a gray one. They bay one was wild, and I couldn't catch it. The other one I caught, cut a limb offen an apple tree, made me a bit out of a piece of it and tied the other end fast, put a couple more strings on the bit and jumped on the horse and rode him down.

You can call it stealin' the horse or not, jest as you're mind to; I took the horse. I rode him about 8 miles down to Craig Claire. Well, I got sick of it, and got some sore ridin' horseback and wasn't used to it. I got off at the end of Craig Claire, got across the Beaverkill River, and I says, "I'll take the bridle off this horse and turn him around and send him up the road." It was gettin' just a bit grey in the East, and I had no time with me at all.

About half past six I rolled into Old Man Green's hotel in Roscoe. I didn't know any of 'em.

The hotel keeper said, "Young man, you rolled in early."

"Yes" I says, "I come up from Beaverkill—Turnwood. I got an uncle that's sick in Sumansville, and I got to git to the road after breakfast."

"All right, we'll have breakfast after a while."

So I went into the house, and I got a drink, a shot of brandy and had a good breakfast. After breakfast, I got a little bottle of whiskey. It cost me a quarter. The breakfast cost me a quarter, two drinks of whiskey cost me 20 cents. Well, I had 2 dollars and 22 cents when I came in. It cost me 70 cents: a breakfast, half a pint of whiskey and two drinks.

"Well," says the hotel keeper, "there's a feller comin' down the road to the acid factory, and he will show you the road that goes across town to Sumansville, if you want to go and see your sick uncle."

Well, the feller come along soon, and the keeper says, "There he's comin' now. He's got a dinner pail." The keeper went out to the porch and told the feller what I wanted.

The feller took me down to the first street I came to and said, "You foller this right out of here. Go across the bridge and go right to Sumansville." Sumansville was formerly Callicoon Center, and I made it there.

When I got to Sumansville I run into a place there—there's a hotel. I thought I'd get a glass of beer. There was three or four travelin' men there. They was drinkin' and raisin' hob, havin' a good time. I told 'em a pitiful story about my uncle bein' sick in Hortonville. Wanted to get the road out there to Hortonville. That was on Callicoon Creek. At Hortonville I would be all fixed to go to Callicoon Depot on the Pennsylvania shore. All I had to do then was to go across the bridge into Pennsylvania. Then I was away from the law altogther.

When I left Sumansville, I was doin' pretty good. I had 6 dollars in money and 2 pints of whiskey them fellers gave me. I got out of there all right, and went to Hortonville, got down to Callicoon Creek. That was about 20 miles from Roscoe. That was four o'clock in the afternoon—a little after— when I was at Callicoon Depot. I went across the bridge, and the tollgate man was at the New York State end of the bridge. He was crippled—name was Knight—Jake Knight. He had a harness shop— was a harness maker and everybody had horses then. Well, he didn't see me, so I didn't have to pay 3 cents to git across the bridge. I got over there and looked around. It was gettin' late, and I said I'd git back and take it slow. I don't believe anybody will ketch me tonight. So I went back to the New York side and stayed all night. I got my night's lodgin' at Hortonville for a dollar and a quarter, and I was pretty well whipped for money then.

I went across the bridge next mornin' about nine o'clock, didn't know whether they'd be waitin' for me with a warrant. Wesley Alden, he was constable, and he had a good team, and he might foller me up. Well, I got across the bridge agin. This time Jake seen me, and I had to pay him 3 cents. You had to pay 5 if you drove a buggy across and 20 for a wagon.

I went across. About 40 feet down below the end of the bridge on the Pennsylvania side was a pine stump. I set on that pine stump. I had a knapsack with my clothes and my butcherin' tools, knives and things and an extra pair of shoes and some socks and a little bit of "soup" [applejack]. I sat down on the stump, jest figurin' out which way to go, up river or down. I was in a strange country, a strange land. But I wasn't dressed too poor or too good. A feller came along, a tall slim man, a little older than I, and he had sandy hair and a big moustache, polite and nice spoken feller. His name was Hiram Conklin. I asked him if he knowed where I'd git a job. He says, "There's lots of work here, if you mind to work."

"Well," I says, "I'll work if I git a job."

He says, "Did you ever lay any stone?"

I says, "Sir, I laid lots of it: field, wall, cellar walls. I laid chimneys."

"Well, all right. You're just the man they want. My brother-in-law and another man, they got a contract here to build half a mile of new road jest below the bridge here, down the crick, right along the bank. They want to lay a retainin' wall."

I said, "What kind of stone?"

He said, "They're drawin' quarry waste, anywhere from an inch and a half to 2 inches thick."

I said, "That's nice stuff to lay."

He said, "You go down with me down here to Tyler's below Callicoon Bridge, about half a mile. I've got to take a cow."

That young cow was the worst thing I ever tried to lead. He had a long rope, and it took us three hours and more to git 2 miles and a half with that cow, and not kill her. Worst, wildest thing I ever seen, sulky and mean. Sometimes she'd go, and sometimes she'd jump and throw herself, raise hob.

We got her home and didn't hurt her. She was some sweaty, and we rubbed her off a bit.

I got the job and worked thirty-four days, and I got a dollar a day and my board. I wrote my father about where I was and what for, and he told me to come back to Dry Brook, and he'd meet me there, and he'd see me about it. Wasn't nothin' to it anyway. I told him I had a good job, and I liked it down there, and I guess I'd better stay a while, and I kept stayin' and stayin', and I got well acquainted and run along three years.

I got acquainted with their cousin, Gordon Conklin, and his second wife. We worked together a lot, dug two or three cellars together. Their grandfather had given Gordon a bear trap—an old homemade bear trap—weighed 50 or 60 pounds. And here the funniest part comes in. The Conklin brothers knowed I was goin' up there a lot and could find the trap and bring it home. I told them fellers where to go, and awful quick.

I never told them the reason I came to Pennsylvania in the first place. They never did know—don't know yet!

After I got through workin' on the road, I got a job cuttin' logs. I lived with the Conklins for three years. Hiram and Gordon Conklin cut logs together. Sherman and Bull Conklin cut together, and Ed and I cut together. Martin was a good feller. He brought the last raft that went down the Delaware River in 1919. They was runnin' some rafts. Hiram, Ed's father, was a steersman. I went on the back end with him. A new hand would go on the back end first and paddle along with the steersman. The back end of the raft was easy enough. The front end was harder. Danger of gettin' knocked off the raft with the oar, especially in rough weather. I got knocked off once in Hanson Eddy on a little teeny raft. I was careless and didn't dip my oars right, didn't have it straight with the way the raft was runnin' and didn't dip it deep enough and let one swell hit another. The thing went right around and throwed me overboard. Old Man Nick hollered for me to hang on the stern and keep my feet out from under the raft. Somebody handed me a pike pole, and I got it, and they jerked me onto the raft. He told me to keep my feet out from under, 'cause he was afraid I'd get them sheared off on a rock.

Rit Appley was an old steersman, and I went with him. He was a hard man to work under; he'd pull you to death. He worked on the river all his life, and he was tough himself, and he thought everybody else was. He wasn't too good an engineer. He didn't know exactly where he was all the time, yet he'd run a raft down the river and had hard work a-doin' it. A lot of 'em were better pilots. They knowed the river better. They pointed a raft better—they called it pointin' 'em. And they knowed how to. Nick Conklin he seed how little he'd pull his oar, and when he did want them to pull, they pulled hard. They wasn't tired out. Hard work. I made sixteen trips, mostly from East Branch to Easton.

I knew Boney Quillen. He was an old man, but he was an awful tough man; sing half the night, make up songs and all that kind of stuff, and the next day it didn't seem to bother him. Like Cage Corbin, he had to have something to drink all the time. He'd go on just as happy.

When I was down there in Pennsylvania, I was stayin' at a place—workin', hayin'—there was a boy about 5 or 6 had hernia. It came on him, and he was screamin' and yellin'; and [then] came an awful rainstorm and an awful flood. It rained that day, hard all day, and there was high water on the river. Well, they didn't have no horse right there, and I said I'd git right down there across to Callicoon and send a doctor up there pretty quick. I told 'em to take the boy and roll him over a keg on his back, carefully bend both ends down a little bit, jest roll him over a keg. I'd heard the doctor tell about doin' that an' runnin' the rupture back by degrees. I ran down across lots, and when I got about the middle of the bridge the water was loppin' right up — pert' near to the planks, within 3 or 4 feet of the planks on the bridge. The Callicoon Bridge was 970 feet long, a plank a foot, I counted 'em — 970. Well I got about the middle, and I looked up the river and seen a big raft comin', a big log raft. No oars on it, no men on it. I run jest as hard as I could to git off the bridge cause I was afraid something was goin' to happen if it'd hit the pier. Maybe knock the bridge off the pier and smash it up. But the raft went right on through, in the raftin' channel, and headed right down the river out of sight. Belonged to a man named Mitchell — Ephram Mitchell up at Hancock. A lot of sawed lumber — he never saw the lumber again, or nothing.

According to John Haynes:

When Mike came back from Pennsylvania, people asked him whether he wasn't scared to ride those big rafts down the river. "Humph," he says, "You're just as safe as if you was in God's pocket."

Once I was on a big log drive in Pennsylvania, drivin' loose logs down the crick 25 miles — the twelve of us. We had two million feet of small pine, peeled, some hemlock peeled—all small logs. The brook wasn't very big, and when the ice went out, floodin' the crick, then they broke some of 'em loose, and they run 'em to the river. Then we'd come back and get another load. Wet to the neck all day and night, we had an awful job. It took us about a month to get two million feet 20 to 25 miles out of there down the river. You'd sleep in wet clothes, go to bed without takin' your boots off. It ain't no good. We had a tent for sleepin', and the fellers came along the shore with somethin' to eat and somethin' to drink and camped in a tent up under some brush. We'd walk along the bank, and sometimes the logs'd get jammed; and we'd have to unjam 'em. That was the dangerous part of it. It took an experienced feller to do that. The fellers have to get on the jam and loosen the key log, then jump off of it and go ahead of it, swim like a son-of-a-gun, go down the river. You'd have to swim out before the logs'd ketch you. You couldn't go up over it. You'd have to go with it, ahead of it, and git away from it, and there was a flood in the crick and wild and woolly and rocky, and there was three or four fellers could do that. I didn't do it.

I done what they called shackin'. When the logs jammed up, a lot of 'em would run out into the woods, and when the jam would go down, they'd leave logs stranded on dry ground. The four of us would each one have a peavey—two hooks on the front end, two on the back—we'd drag it back into the river, wade right down in till it'd float and go back and git another. That was quite a rugged business. 'Course, we had plenty of stimulants all the while.

I was plannin' to marry Nancy Tyler, a nice girl. I worked for her grandfather. He had a sawmill, a water sawmill and a lake. It was run in any kind of weather, any time of year. It was a good wheel, a turbine wheel, and he had custom sawin'. Once he fell on the saw and cut one arm off about halfways to the elbow. He was an old man, his wife died, and Nancy kept house for him. Her and I was engaged to be married in about a month. She had a pet horse — bay horse. He was old and had the blind staggers; they go crazy same as people does with high blood pressure. He went crazy with her goin' down that dugway to Callicoon, and went over the bank and killed her, about a month before we was goin' to be married.

I stayed about two months, and I was about half crazy, kept gettin' worse. The old man was bound I was goin' to stay. He got a woman to do the cookin' — to keep house for him. Bound I should stay. I stayed and finished the sawin' he had in the yard. One mornin' I buckled up my goods in my knapsack, and I walked down to Callicoon. I had a little money, 40 or 50 dollars in money. I got a drink at Brink Pennybacker's. The saloon keeper there let me have a drink or two on Sunday — let me have a pint. I pulled right back the way I went, on foot — walked back to Dry Brook.

When I got back to Dry Brook the people there never knowed where I'd been. I wrote to Hiram Conklin after a while, and I got a letter back. I never seen him again.

7.

ON THE TOWER

When I came back to Dry Brook I was crick watcher for ten years. Now I was on the other side of the fence. I had a lot of trouble; everyone was to work, and there wasn't many local men that done any illegal fishin'. There were young ones — the kids. I had some trouble with Ort Todd's boys, and I had some trouble with Mort Granger's boys and had some trouble to get them to understand they had to stop. I had to stop myself. And the worst job I got into at all, I caught a man that worked for the Goulds for years. Flatfooted him and another feller fishin' in the lake one night. I didn't do anything. He had a family, and he was in debt for a new house, and he used me awful good after that and so did the feller with him. The feller with him was a farmer — Ed Kelly. They're both dead now — Ed Kelly and George Stewart.

Well, I watched crick for ten summers, then I got a chance through the district ranger, Stratton Todd, to go down to the East Branch in the fall. He wanted me to go down, sharpen the tools and help do the drillin'. I done the work, and then we got through the 5th of October, the fall of 1918. The man that was supposed to go on the tower quit, and they asked me to do it. I went on Balsam Mountain with a packload of stuff, a blanket and some food and an old house skeleton key to get in the shanty. I finished the term till the 13th of November. It was an old open tower then—just a water tank but no top on it—cold.

Next spring I wouldn't work for Gould any longer. Stratton Todd was district manager, and I said, "All right, if they're only goin' to pay me for five months a year as crick watcher, I can't live on that. I have got to have a better job, and I'm goin' to quit anyway, go on layin' stone or brick or somethin'. I can get a job in a blacksmith shop, hard work, but I can do it if I have to. I hain't goin' to work any longer on that crick watchin' job. I'm goin' to quit. "Well," he said, "All right." So I was appointed the spring of 1919 fire observer on Balsam Mountain.

Nina Haynes, another acquaintance, commented on this lucky break for Mike:

> The tower job was a godsend for Mike. It done a lot for him. He was the best observer they ever had.

When I was first on the tower, the Director of Lands and Forests, William G. Howard, made a speech at Kingston—at the Stuyvesant Hotel—gave us instructions what to do. We were supposed to report it to the game protector if we observed any infractions of game laws. I didn't agree with that sort of business at all. After a while he changed it, after two years, cause some of 'em got into a squabble about it, and he 'lowed the game protectors should do their work and let us do ours. Those farmers in my town raised cauliflower; and if the deer eat it up and they canned one of 'em once in a while, I didn't care.

I was on Balsam Mountain in dangerous fire weather. Supposed to mail a report once a week. One went to the District Ranger and one went to the Albany office—on wind and weather and the distance you could see and this and that and the other. Fill out the form if you see a fire, what time you saw it, what time you reported it, and who you reported it to, and when the smoke ceased. That was all to go on the report. There was times I was there as much as three or four weeks or more in the spring, when the dangerous fire weather was, and never off the mountain. Somebody would bring grub to me, and every Sunday they'd come with a load. Somebody would come up and bring food and take the reports back and mail them each week.

They missfired sometimes and didn't bring me food. I don't know how, but they missfired and didn't fetch it. They skipped two weeks, and then they skipped another week, and I was scant on food. Then George Lambert's boy brought me a couple of loaves, and I had to go down nights and dig some leeks and eat leeks and bread.

It doesn't get lonesome on the tower—not unless you get half sick or somethin'—or if your telephone goes bad. Then you have to go out and fix it. A telephone is a lot of company. You couldn't rubber, of course, on a high tension line, but at the same time you'd hear rings, and you knowed somebody was alive. That was one thing—I always did kinda like to be alone. And if I lived alone too much, I'd get out and have a good visit, and have a good time, and that'd last for a while. Then I'd go back and stay a week or ten days or two weeks back on the mountain and not mind a bit.

Mike was praised unanimously for his work on the fire tower. Says Waldron Dumond:

> He was a very good scholar, but he lacked school. When he took that conservation job Stratton Todd said he never got a report as good as the one Mike used to put out.

Ed West, a colleague, remembered:

> Mike and I started to work at the Conservation Department at about the same time—in the spring of 1919. He was observer at Balsam Lake Mountain. I was assistant in the survey crew. I got to know Mike very well as time went on. In fact the rangers and observers were at the time asked to help out on survey crews with the cutting of brush on survey lines. I worked for a man named Lawrence McGrath who was in charge of the survey party. When weather would permit and his duties on the mountain would permit, Mike would help us.
>
> It was uncanny how Mike could tell where a fire was in the district, amazing to all of us who knew him. In fact the story was told and retold about how he could spot fires as far away as down in Pennsylvania, when as a matter of fact, the observer on Twaddel Point, which was much nearer the Pennsylvania line, would fail to see it or would miscalculate where it was. On the other hand, Mike could tell exactly where they were, see them plainly, even before the man at Twaddel Point could spot them.
>
> Sometimes when the wind current was in the valley, the fire would be in one place in the valley, and the smoke would be carried along by the wind and rise a mile or two away. When

the smoke would go up he would see the cloud movement and allow for it. Mike had a great reputation for spotting fires with accuracy.

I'd take a sandwich and a bottle of water up there on the tower and stay all day. 'Course I had a telephone up there. As far as I could see, around a circle of 20 miles each way, I knowed the country pretty good. I didn't miss much on the location of fires. I hit 'em pretty good. Now I'm braggin' on myself—don't like to do that but I have to a little. It was so, though. I had some arguments with some fellers. There was one in particular. A new feller down at Twaddel Point, East Branch. That's the valley that comes to Oquago Creek. It runs down to Livingston Manor, if you've ever been down there, and crosses right in the middle and heads back toward Liberty quite a way. Well, the fire wasn't there. It was across the Delaware in the pine woods in Pennsylvania. [District Ranger Leon] Furch asked me, "Mike," he says, "any fire in Bennett Holler?"

"No," I said, "I haven't seen any in Bennett Holler."

"Well," he says, "Bojo does, down in the East Branch."

"Well," I says, "Bojo is wrong. There's no fire there, but across the river, the other side of Cochecton, don't know how fur—there's a turrible smoke across the river in Pennsylvania."

That was after they had the airplanes. They had two up at Troy. Furch didn't say no more. Pretty quick there was an airplane went right over toward Cochecton. It came back and went right back North toward Albany. Well, anyway he got back, and he hollered up to me—telephoned. He said, "Old man, you're right. The fire is about 10 miles from the Delaware River in Pennsylvania."

That stopped Bojo!

When I was fire observer on the State fire tower, there used to be a huckleberry industry in the Shawangunk Mountains above Ellenville. When the crop got down and the berries began to get small, why they'd set the fix according to all accounts and burn over a large territory. One year we had 700 acres of State land burned over, and it cost a lot of money, about 700 men in the woods over a week. One fire I remember well, started a little southeast of Minnewaskey Hotel, burned over a week, an awful territory.

The fire jacks started those fires. They'd set a little candle down on the ground when it was awful dry around it, put leaves and birch bark right up close, then set the candle wick afire and go off and leave it. They'd get quite a ways before it burnt out. The fire fighters found them when they was in the woods fightin' fires. There wasn't much timber on that mountain, just white birch and jack pines, huckleberry brush burnt over; and then the second year after it burnt, you'd have a good crop of huckleberries again.

They caught a feller once settin' a fire. He was the fire observer on Sam's Point. They caught him red-handed settin' fires. His daughter was on the fire station by the telephone, so she could answer calls, and he was runnin' around settin' fires. I can't remember his name. He lost his job, and I don't know whether he's out of jail yet.

As Mike's reputation as a story-teller, fire spotter and naturalist grew, people traveled to Balsam Mountain, not simply for the spectacular view, but because Mike presided over it. Waldron Dumond explained:

When people came up there Mike would entertain them with his stories. He was a noted character for that, and a lot of people went there for the hunting stories. He would have guests register there. Of course, he was only at it eight months a year. He got the great sum of 90 dollars a month.

And John Haynes remembered:

He could tame snowshoe rabbits when he was watchman. He was the only man I know that tamed snowshoe rabbits. Mike would feed them on crumbs, peelings, and so on. I have been there when Mike would go out and holler, "Hey rab, hey rab," and pretty soon they'd come poppin' out of the brush to get the feed.

Waldron continued:

He always told me how rabbits would come out, and he'd feed them. Even, I think he said, he had a partridge. They was the hardest things in the world to tame. 'Course he waged a war on the porcupine. And rightly so. He killed — I can't tell you how many. It was over a hundred one summer. People came to visit him by the hundreds. He was probably the most notable woodsman hereabouts.

Nina Haynes told of her daughter's memorable visit to the tower:

Our two girls came into the house one day and said, "We're going up to see Mike in the tower." I had fried chicken to give them. I said,

"Do you know, it's 6 miles from here to the tower?" They invited three friends along.
Mike was very happy to see them. He met them with open arms. They listened to his stories. They ate his food. He had a meat box. His food was quite tasty. He ate their food, and they ate his. The dogs just sat and watched. The girls offered to do the dishes, but he said, "I'll do them." So he twisted a piece of bread, wiped out the dishes and threw the bread to the dogs. Then he took the girls up to the tower.

There were notable people among Mike's visitors:

I got a story to tell about John Burroughs that happened when I was up on Balsam Mountain. There was two lawyers came here from Newburgh. They had a lot of stuff—thought it would be an awful good job—they was going to change the name of Slide Mountain to Mount Burroughs, 'cause John Burroughs, the naturalist, had put a trail over Slide Mountain from Winnisook Lake and over Cornell and Wittenberg and out in Woodland Valley. Well, that was his favorite trail in the Catskills. He laid it out, and he had a stone bench he built on top of Slide Mountain—there yet, overhanging rock and stones in front. Well them lawyers wanted me to keep that stuff there—a great long string, and have everybody sign it. It was a petition. Well, I didn't think it was a good idea, but I kept it—didn't say nothing to them and didn't ask anybody to sign it. Just a day or two before I left the tower, when I was laid off for the winter, I bundled up their stuff and sent it back to them. I told them if John Burroughs had wanted Slide Mountain named after himself, he would have named it that when he named Slide, 'cause he was the one that named it.

An anecdote published in the Catskill Mountain News *(May 5, 1960) pointed out another famous visitor:*

Nicholas Murray Butler, president of Columbia University, was an admirer of Mike. The story is told that Butler lived atop Balsam Mountain in Mike's cabin for several days, all the time enjoying the mountain wit. After he went home, an acquaintance told Mike just who Mr. Butler was in the field of education. "You mean that school teacher fellow?" said Mike. The reply was, "Yes." "Well," Mike replied, "he knowed more than God Almighty."

It was well known to all who knew him that Mike enjoyed a drink more than now and then. Ed West, when asked about this, replied, "For many years Mike used to be a heavy drinker. They had some great stories about Mike and his drinking. In the last years of his life he gave it up. In his early years he was quite a drinker."

John Asher related that one day Mike had had too much to drink and fell in a deep spring box and couldn't get out. A black servant from the Gould estate, a man named Henry Alexander General George Washington Obediah Knox, came along. Said this awesome gentlemen: "Ah, Mr. Mike, Mr. Mike. You'll drown. You'll drown. Come to me." And he did.

"We'd go up there to his tower, and he'd have a bottle setting around side of him," Ed West continued:

"He'd say, 'Boys, I'd give you a drink, but I want this for my throat.'" Naturally, it interfered with his work at times.

We had a through line, a through telephone line, from Fleischmanns all the way to the top of Balsam Mountain, and Mike was required every day to call in by telephone to find out whether he was all right. If we'd have to find out what was the matter with him, we'd try to call him. On one occasion we didn't hear from him all day and we tried to get him, and the next morning we set out for Balsam Lake Tower—three or four of us from the survey crew and a ranger. We got up to the tower, and Mike wasn't there. And we found him down in some ginmill in Margaretville. Because it was a day or so after pay day, and that trip to the ginmill was more important than being up on the tower, especially since he knew he wasn't needed on the tower, because it wasn't a real fire hazard at the time. I would go so far as to say that had there been a real danger, Mike would never have deserted his post.

Added Ed Lewis:

The last I saw Mike he was down at Bear Mountain. The Department was having a big affair down there. He was there; and of course, naturally, he got loaded.

From the Tower in Winter
Photo by Stuart M. Gross

The Old Wooden Observation Tower (35' high)
from the Forest, Fish and Game Commission
Sixteenth Annual Report, 1911

The Present Tower
Photo by Lyle Baker

Mike's Badge
(1-1/2 x 1-1/2 inches)

Mike in the 1940s
Collection of Betty Baker

8.

MR. BEAR OF THE CATSKILLS

Mike had a way with bears and a way with words. The bear stories, which showed his intimate knowledge of the Catskill forests, made him a regional folk hero.

The main way I learned about the bears was follerin' 'em to see what they're doin', see where they went and remember their runways [the routes bears usually travel]. I had one runway that was fatal for them: when a bear stopped on the top of Double Top Mountain, when they came from the Graham Mountain side, across the head of Beaverkill. They were very apt to stay there in the balsam thicket. Then they'd go on down to the head of Pigeon Brook. I had a three day run, and I'd get a lot of bear by that. Young Frank Fairbairn and I hunted together and he'd never wait. I'd meet him along there. He'd always figure on huntin' the bear. The bear'd go in a hole all the while. I started a lot of 'em up there. I'd meet him, sometimes start to git to the runway, but he'd start the bear through before I could git to the runway. I got provoked after a while and quit huntin' with him.

Uncle Frank was pretty nearly as bad. He was his uncle. But one day him and I brought the bear around the edge of Lon Dury Holler and Graham Mountain. We went across the Dury Ridge and down to the head of the plateau, near the head of the Beaverkill. 'Tain't too far across there, 3, 4 miles come to the level of the notch and see two big mountains there: Double Top and Graham.

"Now," I says to Uncle Frank (we called him uncle, he married my father's cousin), I says, "now here, that bear's going up to the top of Round Top. He'll be up there on the East Deck, or the south end of that mountain probably. I started a lot of 'em off there."

Frank never would wait. I said, "It's cold. We'll build a little fire." We stayed there one hour. Then I said, "I'll hit in around the head of Pigeon Brook. I can get around the end of the mountain and get past the bear." He said, "Ain't no use. Bear will probably go into a hole." I said, "That'll be all right. We can kill him there." I said, "I want to get ahead of him if possible. If there hain't no hole, he'll come right through there, and I know it."

I run about a half dozen through there before that day. Frank didn't stay there too long. He had only about a half mile or so to get to the top of the mountain. It was a cold day. I hadn't been on the runway I don't believe over ten minutes, before I seen the bear comin', a good big bear, and I killed him.

Mike didn't always meet his prey on the open runway:

It must be the best part of fifty years ago. A man by the name of Billy Yorks and Aaron Drake were with me. I was a young lad and so was Aaron — about 18 — and I guess Aaron was a little older and Billy was an older man. We follered an old bear and three clubs in a ledge. The snow was 4 feet deep, and the track was old. We found him after a while, and he wouldn't come out. They'd been in there for a little while, and they got to sleep good and sound—hibernating over the winter—and we had to build a fire in the hole and smoke them to death as we thought they wouldn't come out at all. We shot into the hole and one thing and another, and then Billy Yorks said we got to get him out of there. We figured he was dead because he stopped coughing and so forth. I was the smallest one in the crowd so I was elected to go into the hole with a torch made of birch bark and end him around and drag him part way out to get a rope on him so we could pull him out, and when I got in there I found that one of 'em wasn't dead yet, because I could see his eyes in the dark. That was a kind of interesting time for me to get out of there backwards. We had to do some more smoking and after a while we got him cured and got him out.

One of Mike's most famous stories was that of his eighteen day hunt. James G. Hall, grandson of a close friend of Mike's, Jim Aitkins, remembered it as the Big Hunt: "I. . .used to lie on the floor and listen to he and Mike tell tales about hunting, including the Big Hunt. I was lying on the bear rug which my grandpa had tanned, and this was the bear shot on the eighteen day hunt. Mike Todd stayed at grandpa's house many times, and it was an excuse for us to visit and listen to stories and also stay up late at night."

My longest hunt was started in 1916 on the 16th of December and three of us—Sherwood Samuels, Jim Aitkins and myself—follered that bear eighteen days, and I was on the track the hull eighteen days, and they was on the track sixteen. There was two rainy days that they didn't go into the woods. We struck the bear on the divide between the Beaverkill and the Willowemoc. He had a hole all fixed up there to go in and laid on top of the rock outside of it. He hadn't had anything to eat for several days, and he didn't get anything to eat after. He run right back, he backtracked, and went right off down the Beaverkill and went more'n halfway to French Woods and the Delaware River and back. We raced him twice down there and back and played all kinds of tricks and tried to get ahead of him on the run there, and he'd dodge every time. We didn't get a shot at all, and after a while he had me runnin' up there, and we lost him several times, picked him up and got started again. More snow came and blocked the tracks — a young blizzard. We traveled 18 to 20 miles a day, startin' early in the morning and quittin' at night. Sometimes we'd have to walk to eight or nine o'clock at night to get out of the woods to a place where we stayed. We never did have trouble findin' a place. The Beaverkill used to be full of folks, especially at the upper end of it, and so the Willowemoc and the West Branch of the Neversink. A good many of them are gone now, but in those days there was always folks ready to put us up, and I knew a good many of 'em.

The next morning we'd start up again, going back to the spot where we'd left the bear, and take up the trail.

We ran into another gang of hunters, and one of those fellers throught he was quite slick. They tried to get in ahead of us. I know the country pretty well, if I do say so, and I was right down on my own stampin' ground by now. The other gang went with us one day, and the next day they didn't show up. I said, "They're playin' some shenanigans, and they're goin' to fix to get ahead of us."

I started the bear and gave the others directions where to stand on the runways. The runways are places where bears usually travel. Three runways come off of Eagle Mountain: one at the head of Rider Hollow, one in the Notch, and one down on the Big Indian side. They'd be right there to kill him if he came their way.

I knew pretty well where the bear would lay within a half mile or so, and I then got between the bear and the other gang. That was a trick I could play because I knew the country so well. I follered the bear right over and went over to the other side. There was snow that night. The day before it was raining a bit, and it thawed. It was noisy goin', and I stepped on his track and stepped along easy. Well, I see where he broke off a balsam bush about an inch and a half thick and dragged it into a hollow log to lay on. About the time I discovered him where he was, I turned around to see his head coming out of there, and he got his body out.

Then I shot at him. I had been telling those fellers I was with I was going to point my old gaspipe — that was what I called my rifle — at that bird if I ever see him. When I shot, he never flinched. He went on, and I felt kind of foolish, thinkin' I'd missed him. I couldn't see how I did it, as I figured I could tell within a 4 inch circle where the bullet went in. I overhauled on him and broke his shoulder next time and knocked him down. He went a ways and fell over. The first shot had put a bullet through the side of his heart.

Waldron Dumond hunted with Mike many times:

We used to come up hunting. I lived in Tarrytown, and a friend of mine from Brooklyn, Harry Byrne, he used to come, and we'd go hunting. Camp right below him. We hired Mike, he being a famous bear hunter. We went with him. I remember him distinctly, all the hunts we had.

According to Ed West, Waldron kept a bottle of spirits just for Mike. He had a habit of keeping a bottle in his cupboard with only one or two drinks in it, especially for when Mike would come. Because if he had a full bottle there wouldn't be much chance of getting it away from Mike before the bottle was gone. So Wald had this bottle with a couple of drinks in it especially for Mike.

Waldron carefully admitted that one time Mike got the best of him in this respect:

In the days of prohibition [we] had a place over at Pine Hill where [we] could get applejack. It cost 16 dollars a gallon. I saved money to go over and get a gallon, and I hid it down under the chest, but I hadn't touched it yet. Was saving it for deer season. Mike came in one day and said, "Have you anything to drink?" Those were his first words. Mike loved drink, no question about that. "All right Mike, I got some applejack I'm saving for the deer season, I'll give you a drink." So I gave him a nice generous drink, half a water glass of applejack, worse than whiskey, higher proof. Then he drank that, and he stayed, and stayed and stayed. Finally, he said, "I just guess I'll go down the road to so and so's." And when he had left, I looked at my applejack. It was entirely empty. In three days he emptied that applejack, and my deer season medicine was all gone.

Dave Fairbairn, another bear hunter, and Mike were rivals. Waldron knew and hunted with them both:

> We finally broke off with Mike and got another man because of [Mike's] overindulgence. We got Dave Fairbairn, another bear hunter, because Mike left us once. We were very much disturbed. He had put us on the runway once, at the head of Dry Brook, and he didn't come back. He got down at Big Indian and left us. We didn't care too much for that. It didn't matter too much in our relations, but we did get another man. Mike still came along with us from time to time.
>
> Dave and Mike weren't too friendly. That was jealousy. If I were to make a judgement, Mike killed more bears and was the better hunter of the two, although Dave killed a lot of 'em. But there was a little jealousy between them. I remember coming out of the head of Millbrook one night, and we were tired, had been way out at the head of the Beaverkill and over the head of Millbrook. Coming up on the mountain on the other side, Mike and Dave were ahead. They always wanted to lead, to lead the party and be the boss. Well they were coming out of there at just about dusk, and Dave was ahead. We were 100 yards behind. Mike was going to keep up the pace, and he finally passed Dave. Almost at racehorse speed, but still walking. Finally he got to the top of the ridge. He turned around and said, "There, damn you, Dave, how do you like that?"

Mike also had other ways of amusing himself while he was in the woods. John Haynes related a camp incident that occurred in 1916:

> They was a number of us camped way in the head of Beaverkill. And on this stream was a balsam swamp—a thick swamp. I was coming out of the woods on the opposite side, and I heard this peculiar noise in the swamp. Nothing to be afraid of or to hunt for. I went on to camp. Mike was there. He says, "Do you see anything?"
>
> "No, but I heard something. I heard the funniest noise I ever heard in the woods. It wasn't no bobcat. Wasn't nothing in this woods. But still I don't know what it was."
>
> But Mike had to show me. He didn't want to fool me. He had part of his teeth out, and he'd put his finger in his mouth and cheek, and he'd make the most unearthly noise.

Mike's life was the woods, and he wasn't prepared for participating in the ceremonies devised by civilization. Nate Haynes was there when Mike learned that his father had died. Mike left the deer he had shot hanging on a tree. He told friends that they could have it if they went and got it. This they did, after a great deal of searching. To dress Mike up for the funeral, Nate gave him a coat, someone else gave him a good pair of pants, a third donated a shirt. Thus they dressed him properly for the solemn occasion.

Despite, or perhaps because of, his extensive hunting experience, Mike was humble about his knowledge of the woods:

People say they never get lost, but I've been lost in the woods, but I never get scairt. I've been lost a lot of times when I didn't know where I was at all. One time I followed a bear over to the head of Rondout Crick. I stayed all night under a ledge of rock, it wasn't so cold. The next morning I got up. I couldn't find the bear. So I went down toward the crick. The ledges was awful. I couldn't get down there, it was so awful. So I crawled back up on the ridge and went down the ridge. I came out at Buttermilk Falls, went up by Peekamoose Lake and came down the ridge to the public highway. I went right down the road. I didn't know where I was, and I met a man and asked him if he knowed where I was, 'cause I don't know. "Well," he said, "you're here on the Sundown Road. You go down to the Sundown Post Office." I said, "Is there a road that turns and goes back to the East Branch of the Neversink?" He said "You go down here a ways, take your first road to the right to Red Hill." I went over and down the East Branch of the Neversink, went down that to Claryville. At Claryville I was home. I slept at the hotel. Then I went on and hunted deer for a day or so, and then I went home.

9.

WOMEN IN HIS LIFE

Perhaps out of gentlemanliness, Mike never spoke of the women in his life. And it appeared that the loss of his fiancée in Pennsylvania was something he could not bear to talk about.
According to hearsay, one girl who interested Mike worked in Jerome Moot's Dry Brook store. Waldron Dumond had heard of this liason with Vinnie B.:

Mike had one sweetheart I knew of. She worked for Moot at the general store. They had a spring. It was up on the hill across the brook. A pipe brought the water down to the house. When the leaves in the spring stopped up the pipe, someone had to go up and open it. It was about 200 yards up to the spring. They'd send the hired girl up. So Mike told me he used to go up to the spring and put leaves in the water to plug up the pipe, and then go with the girl to open it up." However, the spring was plugged up so consistently that finally one day Mrs. Moot went to see for herself. . .

It is also rumored that Mike was jilted. According to Nina Haynes:

Mike came in one day—he'd walk into the house most any time. I see his face was really long. I said, "What's the matter?" "Oh, I got something to tell you," he says. "I want you to read this letter." He brought out a letter and let me read it. This girl wrote that she was going to be married soon, and she wanted to be released from marrying Mike. Her father wouldn't let her marry him. She wanted to tell Mike how sorry she was. She was going to be married that day to another guy. Mike was all broke up about it.

There were other relationships, again short-lived, that his acquaintances knew about: a girl named Daisy P. kept house for him one winter, and Mary B. was an outdoor girl who worked at Gould's. But whether by choice or circumstance, it would seem that Mike was essentially a loner.

10.

SKILLS OF A WOODSMAN

The first thing I done when I got off the tower in the fall was to cut down a lot of big poles. Had a nice wood lot of big poles anywhere from 5 to 10 inches through and tall. Well, I cut down about twenty cords, and Lou Kittle would come and draw it out for me, and I'd get stuff and have a good dinner fixed up. Ort Haynes, a cousin of mine, a distant cousin, he had a tractor and a good saw. We'd get up a bee.

In the winter I trapped it mostly, and hunted — hunted foxes. Foxes was wuth money — and bobcats was wuth some money — got a bounty in Ulster County. All the while I lived below George Haynes' place in a little white house in the holler [Millbrook]. I bought the place the year I went on the tower.

I done water witchin'. I'd take a crotched stick — two branches and hold it in my hands — one branch in each hand and hold it right in front of me straight. Then I'd walk slow over the medder or anywhere. Then, when I came over a vein of water the stick would pull right down, and the way that has been proved to be true, we mark the spot and dig the well, sometimes go 20 feet, sometimes 40 or 50 feet, and find a good vein of water.

I used the water beech or witch hazel, apple tree. Other woods, such as maple, work but not as good, but water beech is my preference. It hasn't yet failed to find water where I told it was. I can't tell the depth. Liable to find a better vein in dry seasons than when it is wet. In wet weather you might find a surface vein that will dry up.

I can tell you a good story about water witchin'. It happened last summer, about a year ago now. I think it was the 1st of July, and there was a big flood the year before that wrecked a feller's house. His name was William Ackerley. He lived on the foot of Todd Mountain, and he was going to move his house on a raise of ground 50 rods from where his old house set. Before he moved it, he wanted me to locate him a well — and so I did — and drove the stake right to the side where he was going to dig the cellar, so he could have it beside his house.

Well, the well driller came — set his machine and sighted the drill exactly where I had the stake drove — and he said to me, he says, "How far is it down, Mike?"

I says, "Maybe 100 to 200 feet," but I didn't think it was over 100 feet. I didn't know for certain, but it was a big vein anyway. Well, he started to drill a few days and went down through some gravel and red shale and then had to drive some casings down there 45 feet and struck solid rock. Then three or four days, I went down there in the morning, and he said, "We're going to hit it pretty quick." He drilled about 15 feet and broke right through into a vein of water 2 feet thick. It filled the well two-thirds full in ten minutes. They put in a strong pump, and it never failed. The well was 120 feet deep when it was finished.

Mike also enjoyed practicing his knowledge of home remedies that he learned from his father. Nate Haynes recalled:

> One day, Mike, Charley Todd, and I were going up to hunt deer on a very steep ridge. Charley said, "I'll go up, and you boys make a drive up. Bring the deer through." Before Mike and I started up, Mike wasn't feeling very well. He said, "Before I go I got to get some balsam." He found a balsam tree, and he took his knife, and he cut a slit in the tree, and balsam came out. He rubbed that on his fingers, put it between his eyes and nose, and he was ready to start the hunt.

I was lookin' for bobcats, and I came down into Dyer Hollow, and seen two fellers comin' down out of the mountain with a big horse. They was workin' for the Cruickshanks, at Big Indian. They run a factory down there, a crate factory, made all kinds of crates, gettin' out all kinds of lumber—birch, maple—anything that would make boards. They had worked down there in the woods, and their horse didn't have nothing to drink till noon. He was a nice big horse, about 1500 pounds. The boy rode down into the middle of the crick, and there he drank all the ice cold water he liked. I said, "You want to kill that horse, don't let him drink all that cold water. Better take him over to the house." The house was down the road, and before he got there he was sick in the stomach with colic. I said, "You better take him down to the barn." So he got him down to the barn at George Parson's hotel, the Old Mountain House. He got in the buggy house and got on the floor, and I said, "Don't let him get up. Keep him down, get his harness off. Give him some whiskey, some ginger and warm water in a bottle and pour it down." They wanted to telephone a doctor, and I said, "By the time the doctor gets here he'll be dead." I said, "Get some horse medicine at Bennett's store in Big Indian, Dr. McDonald's Colic Cure. Telephone down to Hiram Cruickshank, tell him to bring up two bottles, No. I and No. 2, and bring 'em up here." This they done and give the horse ginger and liquor to ease him up inside. They kept him down. He kept boltin' and tryin' to get up. He was gettin' well when he got that stuff into his stomach. Then Hiram came, and it said on the bottle give him No. I and in twenty minutes, No. 2. I took about half a bottle and put it down him. Hiram said, "What you going to do, kill him?" I said, "Nope, I think that'll stop that pain, though." When twenty minutes was up, I gave him No. 2, and in ten minutes the horse was cured. He slept for two hours, got up, and then I said, "You want to water a horse after this, take him to the barn and give him some lukewarm water." The owner gave me 10 dollars for saving his horse.

To outsiders, Mike's woodsy appearance was such that he might induce illness rather than cure it. John Asher related:

My wife's mother was born in the Catskill Mountains, and she was a cousin to Mike. Her name was Gwendolyn Haynes, and she married a man by the name of Allen Crumbling from York County, Pennsylvania.

Mike used to let his hair grow down long over his shoulders, and he always carried his rifle everywhere he went. The time my father-in-law come up here to the Catskill Mountains, he dropped up here in a 1925 Buick touring car. As they were going up toward Haynes Hollow Road, Mike appeared onto the road from the woods. Allen, my father-in-law, said to my mother-in-law, "My God, Mom, we're going to be held up and robbed."

My mother-in-law replied to her husband, "No, Allen, that's my cousin, Mike Todd; he won't hurt anyone."

11.

TOO OLD TO WORK

Mike told Waldron Dumond about coming home to the house he owned:

Of course, it might stand there for months closed up. He said, "I went in one night. I thought I'd better go in there. I'd been out the night before, felt awful poor. I had too much to drink," he said, "to be honest with you." He said, "I got in, and I lay down on the couch, and," he said, "there was a wasp flyin' around. It kept gettin' closer to me. I was so weak and bad, that it finally come down on my hand and stung me. You know," he said, "I was so full of alcohol, that wasp just dropped dead, right in the middle of the table."

Mike had the habit in later years of coming off the tower in the fall and staying at various houses in Dry Brook. That was all right for a week, people liked to have him, but when it went on for three weeks, it got tedious. The whole problem of where to stay loomed up.

Ed Lewis described the situation at the time of Mike's retirement from the tower:

He couldn't manage any more. He couldn't take it, but they let him stay on. He was such a good man at one time, and they let him stay on. I used to cover for him.

In 1947 I was 70 years old, and I had to retire. I was gettin' so I wasn't able to cart my grub on the mountain good—it took me half a day to get there—it was gettin' a little tough. I had my place paid for, I could do something else. I worked some for young Kingdon Gould, got my little pension from the State, trapped a little, shot myself some unlawful meat, and so forth.

I stayed with some neighbors. I stayed there for five years, paid 'em a dollar and a half a day for board. Got a little pension and got the rest from the County. But in the first place I sold my place for 2,000 dollars. It cost me 200 dollars for the real estate agent and then the lawyer charged me for searching the title. He picked up 30 odd more. Well, then I had to pay income taxes, and I owed a little, some bills. I paid everything and put the rest of the money in the bank. But if I had been a bit brighter than I was, I'd have put that in somebody's safe. If I had not put it in the bank, then I'd have kept my money. I found that out later. But I had the money in the bank, and the County found out where it was so I couldn't go back to it. Well, I paid my board out of that till it was gone, and then I git a little pension from the State, 'bout half of what I should git, accordin' to what I had done. They cut me out of time. Commissioner Duryea put down—I got it in print—twenty- eight years actual services fur the State, but when he went out of office and William G. Howard was director of Lands and Forests and Keeney was his deputy, well they was all set and I got—besides what retirement fund I got—$17 a month—I got $54.70 a month. But jes' as quick as they died off and Duryea quit, they cut my pension down to $25 a month. Then I had to go on the County, and I stayed at the neighbors'. I got sick of it, awful sick. I went to another place, and couldn't take it thar.

Waldron Dumond echoed the problem of the lonely old man without home or family:

This whole problem of where to stay always came up. Mike, of course, had a little place up on the Millbrook Road. Then he sold that. That left him with nowhere.

12.

YARNS OF A CATSKILL WOODSMAN

Cage Corbin, Stagecoach Driver

Cage Corbin, a comical feller, drove a stagecoach from Delhi to Kingston. On the way Cage used to stop at all the taverns, and sometimes they'd have to tie him to the stage after he'd been drinkin' to keep him from fallin' off. He'd gather up the reins of his four-horse team, run a figure eight right out on the street. Then somebody'd throw down a silver dollar and he'd turn over the dollar with his wheel right on the edge of it. He'd run to the depot and holler, "All aboard," and they figured that he could drive safely after all that. All the businessmen along the road would trust him, too, and send their money to the Kingston bank with him.

They had tollgates along the turnpike every few miles. The stage company paid its tolls quarterly. They were behind in payments, and a little down below Margaretville the tollkeeper wouldn't let Cage through. So he unhooked his leaders, took a chain and tore the gate right off and drug it out of the way. Then he hooked up his team and went on.

One winter night it was drifted pretty bad, and Cage couldn't see the road. He was on top of Palmer Hill near Andes, and he left the highway and started right across the fields. Some passenger asked, "Do you know this road?"

"Yes, yes," he answered, "I know every rock in this field."

Pretty quick he hit a big rock and the coach upset.

"There, be Jesus," he said, "is one of 'em."

Yes sir, this Corbin was a comical feller. On the 4th of July he used to dress up in a winter suit and vest, wear a straw hat with no top with his hair standing on end, and in broad daylight he'd carry a lighted lantern.

•

Cage Corbin was a great rangeman and a great horseman. He worked on the Delhi Stage, Delhi to Kingston for years, and then that run down and stopped after a while. He was an old man, but he was a powerful man. I guess his father was a lawyer, and he got mixed up in that Anti-Rent business — was on the landlord's side of it — Cage's father, Tim Corbin. Well, Cage was drivin' stage, two teams and one wagon, he'd go down one day and back the next from Downsville to Arkville. I know. I stayed on with him. Well, sometimes along in that season when he was driving that stage, he would stop in Arena and stayed all night on some occasions. There was a feller there that tried to abuse him, called him one thing or another, called him a coachman and a drunk, and twitted him about his father being tarred and feathered by the Indians, the Down-Renters. Because he was in favor of the rent fellers, they tarred and feathered him, and Will Brisbane made up a song about him, and the man sang this song. It made Cage pretty mad, an old man he was and a powerful man. He didn't like it at all. He got up, actin' just as he was goin' to leave this place, and he collared this feller and shook him till he whimpered like a sick pup, and Cage says, "If my fingers hadn't slipped off, I'd have broken your damn neck."

•

Once he was on the line going to Delhi, and he stopped at what we called the Factory to change horses, or something, and he was pretty well loaded with liquor, drunk. He drinked a lot anyway. He got off, and they changed his team. There was a feller there wanted to be smart, and he jumped on the stage and started his team and left Cage there. Cage, he begin to holler "HAW." And he called the leaders by name. One was Jerry, and one was Jack. "Come here, haw back, come here, Jerry and Jack." And they turned right around with the stage in spite of the other driver and come back to him, right in the stable.

Poachers

Old Man Ruff had a lot of land on the West Branch of the Neversink. He was an Englishman and pretty hard on poachers. There was an old man and his son who lived on Hunter Mountain by the name of Jack and Beebe Smith. They was good men with rifles, and they used them somewhat careless sometimes. Well, they got into an argument with crick watchers on Old Man Ruff's land one day. So one morning Old Man Ruff was out fishin' with a fly, and CRACK went a rifle, and his fishpole fell right in two. He was in a fix for a while. He got another fishpole, and in a day or two he was fishin' again, and the same thing happened. It was a fact, too, because Old Man Ruff told me so himself.

•

Ed Burhans was one of the first game protectors appointed by Governor Hill, and he went up to see Smith because there was a lot of partridges snared, and Ed wanted to get evidence on somebody. He had a bottle of whiskey, and he went to the door and knocked. The woman come and opened the door, and he spoke to her and asked if her husband was home. She was sitting there with a Winchester rifle, a 30-30, in her hand, and she asked him what he wanted. He said he'd come up to give the boys a drink and talk to them a while. She said for him to set it right there on the door sill and leave this place just as quick as you can. So that's what he done.

I was in that myself a little when Joe DeSilva was game protector. He and I was always good friends, and he asked me quite a little to do some spying for him. I asked him whether he had a grudge against me. "What do you mean?" he said.

I said, "If I took that job in this country, I'd get shot."

A Bark Peeler's Life

They peeled a lot of bark for the tanneries in the old days. That was hard work. Men worked 15 to 16 hours a day in the bark woods—from sun to sun was the rule. The men got covered from head to foot with the sticky sap from the hemlock trees. I see 'em just as sticky, you'd take off a pair of overalls and let 'em dry, and they'd stand up by themselves. It was the spring of the year, and another thing they had a lot of trouble with in the bark woods was the gnats—"no-see-ums." They'd just kill you in warm and cloudy weather. You'd daub your face with kerosene and tar. In the shanties they'd use smoke—a house full of smoke to drive out the gnats.

Contractors would hire a gang of men to peel bark, and there was a man down around Shandaken that had about a dozen workin' for him and livin' in a shanty. His name was Conrad. He didn't feed 'em too good, and they had a lot of bad butter. It didn't smell too good, and it didn't taste too good. So they made it up that Judd Todd—he was one of twelve sons—would ask the blessin' at the dinner table. He got down to the table and he says:
Oh, Lord of Love,
Look down from above
And give us something better.
We're crammed and jammed and daily damned
With Conrad's stinking butter.

Saved by a Bark-Peeling Spud

This is a story handed down by my father and from my grandfather to him:

There was a colored man named George Cannide who was an escaped slave, they said. He came to Kingston, kept drifting by hook or crook and stayed at the Parker's at Big Indian. George finally left the Parker's and crossed the mountain to Dry Brook to work for Grandfather Todd in haying. He'd go back and forth over the mountain, and he once went over in the winter to get his bark spud because he had a job to come over and peel bark for Old Man Hiram Graham the next summer. On his way back with the bark spud a drove of wolves got after him. It was night—moonlight night—and he couldn't climb a tree, or he'd freeze to death, it was so cold.

He knowed where there was a holler tree stump 8 or 9 feet high. A part of the tree had split off, and he could get into the half circle and defend himself. He jumped in, and they couldn't get in behind him, and he killed five wolves with that bark spud. A bark spud is a wicked thing, a good heavy one with a blade onto it.

Shenanigans at a Skimmelton[1]

When a couple'd get married they'd raise hob—sometimes take 'em right out of bed at night. I and

---

1 A skimmerton, in this case, a charivari or shivaree.

a feller carried an anvil weighing 150 pounds about 2 miles to a place where they was going to have a skimmelton. On the bottom of the anvil was a hole into it about an inch square. It had been drilled deep in there. Then we'd take a hardwood board and make a plug for the hole and take a chisel and gouge into the plug so we could put a fuse in and fill it full of blasting powder. Then put the plug right back in there and set the fuse off. Frank Fairbairn — a young lad a year older than I — we took it back of the house and set in on a wagon right under a winder thinkin' we'd be smart and set it off. We had an old wet bag to throw over the anvil so they couldn't see the sparkle of the fuse inside the house. The man opened the winder and stuck his head out just about ten or fifteen seconds before it went off. I was standing there with the wet bag and throwed it in the man's face and knocked him right back out of that winder, and about that time, WHANG, it went off and knocked every glass out of the winder. It was a close shave for him.

The Minister and the Calf

There was a minister got all ready to go to church, a friend of mine. He forgot he had a calf that had to eat. The milk was on the stove already warm, so he went out to feed the calf. He was all dressed for church. He got the milk, and the calf gave a slap and spilled the milk all over him. That made him out of sorts, some, and he said, "If I wasn't a minister of the gospel and a lover of the Lord, Jesus Christ, I'd knock your goddamned head right through the bottom of that pail."

Closest to the Fire

This ain't no tale—it's a true story, very near as old as I am, but not quite. It happened in Delhi. An agent named Lyons traveled around on horseback taking orders for everything: orders for hardware, groceries, clothing stores. He even took orders for fruit trees.

Well, this fall Lyons came to a hotel in Delhi durin' court week. Delhi is the county seat of Delaware County. He was wet and cold, and he came into the main room and found a gang of lawyers seated around the fireplace. They wouldn't give Lyons a seat near the fire, so he sat off to one side.

The lawyers started asking questions of one thing or the other. They said, "You travel all over the State, what's the custom in Unadilla?" Another asked, "What's the custom in Roxbury, Hobart?" They were making fun of him. One feller thought he'd be a little smarter than the rest. He said, "You've been all over the State. What's the custom in Hell?"

Lyons said, "They're just about the same as they are here—all the lawyers closest to the fire!"

•

In the fall of the year, hotel men would get a barrel of oysters in the half shell. Old Man Lyons asked a clerk if he had any oysters in the half shell around.

"Yes, yes," said the clerk.

"Now you do as I tell you. I'm paying for the oysters. Take the oysters out to the barn and feed them to my horse." So the clerk got the oysters and went back to the barn. The lawyers all went out to see the horse eat oysters in shell. Of course, the horse wouldn't touch 'em.

Clerk came back disgusted. "The horse won't touch 'em."

Lyons in the meantime had spread his coat out on some chairs to dry and took the best seat—right in front of the fireplace. He set right there, getting warm and dry. So when the clerk came back and said, "The horse won't touch 'em," Lyons said, "Well, if you please, bring 'em right here, I will."

A Fish Story

An old feller went along the highway right alongside the river. And a young feller set there fishin'. The old man asked the young feller had he had any luck. The young un said, "No, not today, but the other day I was fishing here by the deep hole, and I caught a black bass 36 inches long. Have you been fishin'?"

It takes an awful big one to be 18 inches long, so the old man said, "Yes, I was up here by the rocks in the deep hole. I got my line snagged and I pulled and pulled, and after a while I pulled up a lantern— all lit. It had been burnin' all night."

"You old liar!" says the young man. "What you telling me such a story as that for?"

"Tell you what," the old man said, "If you'll take 18 inches off that bass, I'll blow out the lantern."

Fast Work in the Oats Field

I had a big field of oats cut down. There was apple trees down through the field, and I made a bet with a man that was there. I told this feller I'd bet him a dollar that I could rake up two sheaves of oats and make two bands and tie one and throw it up in the air and tie the other up before the first struck the ground.

He 'lowed he'd bet the other dollar, so we bet. I raked up the two sheaves side by side close to the apple trees. So I tied one sheaf and threw it right up in the top of the apple tree and then tied the other one before he could get the first one down out of the tree.

Grandfather Todd

Grandfather Todd was quite a feller, I guess, justice of the peace a long while. He'd law himself right out of the country. Yes sir, him and a feller had farms that jined right above the other. The other feller had a big spring of water that run right down on grandfather's land, and they got into an argument over it. Grandfather had very little to do but dig a ditch and run the water down side of his land through a gully so it didn't run across his medder. But, instead, he took it to a lawsuit, and both of 'em lawed a mortgage on their places.

Uncle Rube's Headache

George Gould—Old Man Jay Gould's son—was visiting with Uncle Rube Todd over by Furlough Lake. Uncle Rube told about huntin' bear and foxes. He was quite a hunter and he told about killin' a bear. He told the truth, but George Gould wouldn't believe him. So George Gould told about huntin' prairie chicken out West someplace. Gould said he killed 100 prairie chickens before ten o'clock in the mornin'.

Rube's father-in-law was listenin', and he sees Uncle Rube shake his head—he didn't believe the story. So he says, "Mr. Todd don't seem to believe the story."

Uncle Rube said, "Don't doubt the truth of the story a damn bit, but it hurts my head to believe it."

I Came Back Alive

His name was Turner. He worked in an insurance office somewhere in New York City. He's shot in a shootin' gallery a lot and one thing or the other. He had a good rifle, and he'd shoot it, too good to suit me. He was a great feller to imagine a lot of things. Snow was about 6 inches deep, a little light crust on it, just a little—could throw a match through it almost—cold, a little snow flying. We went up an old tote road to go over the head of the Beaverkill lookin' for backtrack. He'd see a leaf flyin' along on the crust of the snow, a leaf off a beech bush, and go shootin' like a blue streak, SLAMMETY WHANG. That was interesting to me. I stayed behind him. I said to myself, "Bud, I'm going to play a joke on you before long."

We went right on down to Reed Swamp, and there was no track. We went right up to the Beaverkill, to the turn of the crick. I call it Square Elbow—runs right back north—heads between two mountains, Double Top and Graham. There is a swamp about half a mile long above the turn of the crick. Took him up to the south end of the swamp and left him. I said, "You sit right here, and I'll muck something out of there to you." I didn't have the slightest idea when I left him whether I was ever going to see him again.

It was about two o'clock when I left—half past one. I know he was cold and couldn't stay long. He knew enough to foller my track home. After dusk he came, and he was the maddest man you ever see—but I was alive.

The Woods is Full of 'Em

One day an old man was cuttin' wood up in Deep Holler Notch. The old feller was deaf. A city feller came along. He was all dressed up in fancy huntin' clothes—carryin' a gun. He asked the old feller, "How far is it to Hunter?"

The old man said, "When I came up here a big drove of partridges flew right across the crick into the bush there."

The city feller said, "I don't care about that. I want to know how far it is to Hunter."

"Well, I went after a pail," the old man said, "and I scairt up another drove, and they went right across the crick."

The city feller said, "You're pret' near a damn fool."

"Yes," the old man said, "the woods is full of 'em."

I Came Back Home to the Catskills

I worked in Norwich for one year and ten months in a stone mill sharpenin' stone tools. It was gettin' toward the 1st of November, and I wanted to go huntin'. I wanted to get home to the Catskills and hunt a little bear and deer. I asked the boss—Jack Hogan—to let me off for two months. I wanted to get away from the smell of the blacksmith shop. "Oh, no, " he said, "no, no, you can't go that long, but I'll let you go two weeks."

On Monday morning I went to the bank and got what money I had and took my sachel and clothes and my gun and went down to the depot and come back home to the Catskills, I got home all right, and I ain't seen the boss since—never went back.

The water there was miserable and warm—had to drink beer all the while—got tired of that, too. So I came back to the Catskills and haven't been out since. Ain't seen Jack Hogan fifty years.

Out of the Lion's Mouth

Uncle Jim Todd bought 160 acres from Armstrong. He paid $1,000 plus 10% interest for ten years. Wasn't allowed to pay it off beforehand. Uncle Jim at last got the money and went to the city to pay off Armstrong. Armstrong returned with Uncle Jim to the depot. He wished him luck and asked him to come see him sometimes.

Uncle Jim says, "I'm out of the lion's mouth, and I hope to Jesus Christ I never lay eyes on you as long as I live."

Uncle Jim Goes to Oregon

For years before the Conservation Department was started these settlers on the West Branch of the Neversink, Beaverkill, and Big Indian had sawmills. There were one or two of these mills in every neighborhood. The timber on the State land didn't have no one to enforce the law on it, and they cut the timber on the State land just as they had a mind to. A feller owned a lot of timber would take off his first. He would just keep cuttin' back on the State land.

When David B. Hill was elected Governor of the State of New York, he appointed twelve game protectors and forest rangers. And they began lookin' around Big Indian Valley for violations on State land. Uncle Jim was down to his two daughters in Oliverea. He wasn't any worse than any of the rest, but he got his share of the timber off the State land. When he heard that they were goin' to get after them all, he sat down, stroked his long white whiskers a little bit and told his son-in-law down there, he 'lowed he'd go to Oregon. He had some relatives there. He guessed he'd visit.

Shooting a Skunk

A feller by the name of Clancy used to run a barber shop and a gin mill here in Phoenicia. He bought a piece of property of Charley Ford, and there was all kinds of stories about it one way or the other. But anyway, Clancy signed his papers, and he got it straightened up.

Charley Ford didn't like it, and he wanted his money back, his papers back and so on. So, Clancy goes and gets his shotgun and went down and shoots Ford and killed him. Came pert' near killin' Frank Tyler too—shot two shots of buckshot through his coat. On his way home Clancy met a feller used to be a forest ranger down here—Dave Hilton—and he hated Dave on sight. Dave said, "What you been huntin?" He says, "I just killed a skunk down here," and, he says, "I'd just as soon kill another as not." Dave went right on and didn't ask any more questions.

Hunting in the North Woods

There was three fellers went up in the north woods deer and bear hunting. They got a cabin, got moved in O.K., and the first mornin' after they got all set, it rained all mornin' and cleared off after dinner. One of the fellers did go out to see what he could find without the guide, and he ran into an old bear and three cubs. He started to shoot. The old bear pitched after him. He ran for the cabin. When he got there the door stood open. He got within his length or a little more, stubbed his toe on a rock and fell, his head close to the open door. The old bear was close behind him, jumped over him and went right into the cabin with the other two fellers. The first feller jumped up and jerked the door shut and yelped out. He says, "There, you fellows can have that one. I will go back and get me another!"

Belcher's Band

Close to seventy years ago there was a Belcher's Band, four brothers. The leader was Alny Belcher. There were seven in the band. The others were also Negroes, but not related. Jim Brunt—oh, what a man he was with the violin. First colored men I ever seen was Belcher's Band. Belcher owned a large farm up in Terry Clove above Downsville. The old Belcher homestead still stands there—the original house still stands. The band played at the 4th of July celebrations in Margaretville on an outdoor platform. They played at celebrations and at house dances. There were quite a few Negro families in Delhi. After the band broke up and he left the farm, Alny Belcher went to Delhi and spent his last days there. He was born in '48.

APPENDIX 1

"STOP THIS BEAR HUNT"

Reprinted from the *Catskill Mountain News*
Margaretville, New York, June, 1958
by permission

Mike Todd, 80 years of age, lifelong resident of Dry Brook, bear hunter, fire tower watchman, dry wit with many stories of the forest where he was reared and spent his life, writes *The News* from Dale's Sanatorium, Saugerties, where he spent the winter.

He tells about a bear hunt which took place in the last half of November many years ago. He says, "It was the worst night I ever spent in the open." The story runs along:

George Lambert was caretaker at Balsam Lake Club. He and I started to go over to the Willowemoc to see Chet Bisley. George had some business with him. But we never got there. We found a bear track in the Murray Brook hollow. The snow was about eight inches deep. There was a thin crust which made the walking noisy.

There was a good crop of beechnuts, many of them hung in the burr 'till late. The bear whose track we found had been running all over the hollow picking beechnuts off the crust ahead of him.

We followed him around. I though we might get a shot. But we didn't. It was late in the afternoon when we found an old bear track made when the snow was soft about five days before. I told George we would follow the old track. He didn't like leaving the new track for the old. He had never hunted bear anyway. I told him we might as well follow a railroad track as that fresh bear track because he was feeding and would not go in a hole of a hollow tree for several days. But we might find the other bear holed up.

So we went on the old track. About sundown I noticed that George was becoming tired. We climbed out of the hollow toward the Beaverkill. It was steep and leggy. We kept going until we found a ledge with a good overhang. I gathered bark and dry wood and started a fire in front of the ledge.

We stayed there all night. We had brought bread and chunks of meat from home. We had no axe or basin to make a hot drink, icicles for water. We froze on one side and burnt on the other, never slept a wink.

But we started early next morning after the bear. We followed the track over into the head of No. 10 Hollow which is a branch of the Beaverkill, then down into the hollow where the bear came to a spring and followed down the brook which led from it.

I knew the sign and told George, "That lad is not going far before he holes up." When the bear came out of the brook he began back tracking in the hope of fooling us in addition to walking down the creek.

A distance further on he had dragged brush into a bear-sized hole under a big rock. When we were about 100 feet from the rock I told George to stay there and be ready. I would slip around the big rock because I thought there might be a hole through on the other side.

I got around the rock OK and found a hole. I yelled to George "look out." When I yelled, the bear started out of the hole toward George. George shot him through the nose. Then the bear turned and came my way. I hit him a bit higher up in his face and finished him.

We dragged the bear down to the Beaverkill and to an old road which used to go through to Claryville. We left him there and went to Balsam Lake about 2-1/2 miles away.

We were two tired lads when we got there, washed up and George found a full quart of Old Crow. I am telling you, we soon lowered the contents of that bottle.

The night we had the fire in front of the ledge Mrs. Lambert told us was 16 below zero. Young George Lambert took a team and sled to bring the bear which weighed 182 pounds. This story is all straight goods.

APPENDIX 2

THE LAST YEARS

Camp Woodland gave Mike renewed contact with his own roots. Here were people who genuinely respected him for what he was and found a functional place for him in the little world they had created in the Catskills. They were people who cherished all his accomplishments and skills: his knowledge of weaving and dyeing, his story-telling, his musicianship, his knowledge of the woods. His whole experience was not only valued; it was put to work on a daily basis, and he again became a useful member of society, needed and wanted.

Mike embraced the opportunities wholeheartedly. He was self-motivated and found many important places where he could be very useful as he continued his lifelong avocation of explaining the woodsman's life to city people. He was ready whenever needed to talk to campers about hiking, building fires in the forest, protecting food against animals, finding one's way when lost, and many other bits of woods wisdom.

He introduced the campers to many ancient arts. One such was lining bees. Sometimes he could be seen standing near the camp road, a bowl of sweetened water on a stand nearby. He watched the bees as they swooped down for a drink of the water, circled heavily about, and made a bee line for their hive, hidden in some hollow tree in the woods. He would then move the bowl of water, watch the bees as they flew from the new point, and after establishing a number of lines of flight, he was able to follow and discover the hidden hive.

Mike was fond of demonstrating the obsolete craft of shaving hoops for kegs and barrels. Mr. Hallenbeck, the sawmill man, made a hoopshaving horse after Mike's plans. This and a complete set of cooper's tools were housed in the museum. Mike also helped the campers to learn weaving and dyeing using local wool and plants. His skill at prospecting for water veins with a willow wand convinced all of the validity of water witching. Every Friday night found Mike at the square dance led by George Van Kleeck who played the accordian and knew an amazing number of old Catskill calls. Mike accompanied with his harmonica and bones. He also introduced the washtub drum which many campers learned to play.

Whatever Mike did, his love of the children and his ability to communicate with them was profound.

APPENDIX 3

A REAL MOUNTAIN MAN

Death Ends Story-Telling
And Exploits of Mike Todd

Obituary from the *Catskill Mountain News*
May 6, 1960. Used by permission.

Merwin Todd, top bear hunter of the Catskills, familiarly known throughout the region as "Mike," died Friday in the Margaretville hospital after a long illness, part of which had been spent in a convalescent home in Saugerties.

His funeral was held on Monday at the Herrick funeral home in this village. Rev. George Gevert of the Methodist church officiated. Internment was made in the family plot at the Clovesville cemetery.

"Mike" was born in upper Dry Brook nearly 83 years ago. He would have reached that age in September. His life had been spent in this section with the exception of a few years at Saugerties. He was the son of Hiram B. Todd and his wife, Elizabeth Ganoung [sic].

Mike did not secure a school education. But he was a keen and observant man who put his wits to good use whether fire tower watcher, lumberman, bear hunter, blacksmith, fire warden, amateur veterinarian, stone mason or whatever skill he undertook...

The countryside is full of [Mike's stories]. We recall the time he was compelled to buy a pair of shoes from the Conservation Department. An offical visiting with him one day asked how Mike liked the shoes. "Got my feet wet walking through a covered bridge," was his reply.

Walking down Dry Brook one day years ago a friend asked, "Where are you going Mike?" "Down to Margaretville to git drunk and how in h-- I dread it," was his quick answer.

One Sunday years ago he attended a dinner where a fight developed, heads were targets, two or three of the combatants had to be hospitalized. "How did you like the fight?" he was asked next day. "D-- savage entertainment" came his reply.

Many a time Mike had followed a bear for a week, sleeping in the open, having little food. But it is said he always got his bear. He had killed a large number, probably is best known as a bear hunter. On one expedition with a side-kick the two came to a cave. Mike's companion dropped down into the cave to ascertain if the bear had "gone in." It had. He shouted to Mike, "Here's that bar, come down and help." Mike knew two men in a bear cave was one too many. He called back "You and the bear fight it out."

Mike is survived by a brother, Gerald V. Todd of New Berlin, several nephews and nieces. In attendance at the funeral from out of this section were Mr. and Mrs. Gerald V. Todd, Lee Starr, Mrs. Russell Todd, Mr. and Mrs. Douglas Bice and daughter, Mrs. Arthur Smith, all of New Berlin; Mrs. Clarence Palmer of Norwich.

Photo by Herbert Haufrecht

APPENDIX 4

NOTES

The people whose anecdotes were quoted in this book knew Mike Todd during significant periods of his life. A few knew him as a boy and young man; others knew only the older man. Two of them worked with him when he was observer on Balsam Lake Mountain tower. Most of those interviewed were relatives, some of them very distant. I interviewed them all with a tape recorder.

The first person I knew in Dry Brook Valley, aside from Mike himself, was Lena Knapp Haynes, second wife of John D. Haynes. We met her in the late fifties when we visited Dry Brook with carloads of Camp Woodland young people. The Haynes then lived in the Moot house, which, in the old days, had been a general store with a large room upstairs where the governing body of the Town of Hardenburgh held its meetings. She was a gracious person and entertained groups of our visiting campers every summer with stories of Dry Brook history. Upstairs she took us through the little museum of memorabilia that she had collected. We held our first interview there with her husband, John, on August 5, 1978. Mike had died quite recently and I had written "All the Homespun

Days," a memorial poem. I had taken down the story of his life and wished to supplement it with the remembrances of people who had known him. On August 23rd I had an interview with Nora Graham Baker on the history of Dry Brook.

In 1963 I interviewed Robert Fairbairn, a distant relative, who had gone to the little red schoolhouse in the valley with Mike and remembered him well from those days. From then on there were long intervals between interviews. Camp Woodland ceased to exist in 1962, and my summers roaming through the Catskills ceased. New York City was my base, and I was busy directing Downtown Community School. During the summers my wife and I satisfied our long-withheld desire to travel. All during the years from the first interview in 1960 to the last ones in 1978 I was nagged with an inner voice that demanded that I finish the job.

On July 3, 1965 I interviewed Waldron Dumond in his little cottage near Dry Brook, far up the valley. He was of Huguenot descent, from a family that had moved into the area before the Revolution. Waldron taught school in the Catskills and then in Westchester county. He knew Mike intimately for many years.

By 1970 my good friend Lena Haynes had moved from the Catskill area to a nursing home in Connecticut. I wrote a letter to the local paper, the *Catskill Mountain News*, asking for people who knew Mike Todd. From that letter came an interview with Orson Haynes and his wife, Nina. By the time I came back for the second interview, Orson had died. On October 15, 1973, I taped an interview with Nina Haynes.

Orson Haynes was a brother of John Haynes; I interviewed a third brother, Nate, with his wife in

1978. In 1978 I also interviewed Mary Haynes Liddle, daughter of John Haynes by his first wife. The Haynes brothers were third cousins of Mike Todd. They also had sharp memories of him.

In 1973 I also interviewed Ed West and Ed Lewis. They were not relatives of Mike's, but were among his co-workers at the State Department of Conservation. Ed West was a surveyor and an authority on land titles in the Catskills. Ed Lewis was a fellow observer. When I interviewed him, he was retired. I had known him in the fifties when he was observer at Red Hill, where groups of campers from Woodland would visit him in his tower.

In addition to Nate Haynes and Mary Liddle, I interviewed some other people in 1978, for example, Stratton Todd, the grandson of the Stratton Todd who gave Mike the job on the tower, and his son, Roy. At the same time I interviewed Cecil Polley, an 86-year old retired businessman in Margaretville. He hunted with Mike for many years and had interesting stories. He is of no relation to Mike.

Another important person in the history of these interviews is John Asher. He is a distant relative of Mike's by marriage and came from Ohio to Dry Brook thirty years ago. He visited Mike at Dale's Sanitorium in Saugerties and was instrumental in having the sick old man brought back to die in his native Dry Brook.

Other who contributed their remembrances are Gwendolyn Haynes Crumbling, Jean Haynes Finch, Mary Bogardus, James Hall, Mildred Fairbairn, and John Fairbairn.

INDEX

A
Ackerley, William 31, 84
Aitkins, Jim 74
Alden, Wesley 50
Alder Lake 33, 40
Anderson, Will 22
Andes 92
Animal doctoring 18, 86
Anti-Rent War 25-27, 92-93
Applejack 51, 77-78
Appley, Rit 53
Arena 92
Arkville 92
Armstrong 103-104
Asher, John 12, 31, 86

B
Baker, Nora 26
Balsam 28, 85
Balsam Lake 109
Balsam Lake Club 42, 107
Balsam [Lake] Mountain 7, 28, 37, 58-60, 63-64, 66
Banjo 33
Bark peeling 95
Bear hunting 28-30, 72-76, 78, 80, 105-109, 113
Bear Mountain 66
Bear traps 47, 52
Beaverkill 40, 49, 72-73, 75, 102, 104, 108-109
Bees 110-111
Belcher's Band 106
Belcher, Alny 106
Betting 100
Bice, Mr. and Mrs. Douglas 114
Big Hunt, The 74-75
Big Indian 21, 76, 78, 86, 96, 104
Blacks in the Catskills 96, 106
Blish, John 41-42
Bogardus, Mary 16
Bojo 61-62
Bones 33-34
Brisbane, Will 92-93
Brown, Henry 24
Brunson, Betsy 15-16
Brunt, Jim 106
Burhans, Ed 32, 94
Burnham Hollow 21
Burroughs, John 64
Butchering 20
Butler, Nicholas Murray 65
Buttermilk Falls 80
Byrne, Harry 77

C
Callicoon 54, 56
Callicoon Bridge 51
Callicoon Center 49
Callicoon Creek 50
Callicoon Depot 50
Cannide, George 96
Camp Woodland 1, 3-9, 110-111
Cat's Ladder 48
Catskill Mountain News 65, 107, 112
Christians, Old Man 47
Civil War 29
Clancy 105
Clark farm 12-14, 16, 19
Clark, Jim 13
Claryville 80, 109
Cochecton 61
Columbia University 65
Combat, George 33
Conklin, Bull 52
Conklin, Ed 52
Conklin, Gordon 52
Conklin, Hiram 51, 52, 56
Conklin, Martin 52
Conklin, Nick 53
Conklin, Sherman 52
Conrad 95
Conservation Department 66, 104, 113
Cook, Old Man 42
Corbin, Cage 53, 91-93

119

Corbin, Tim 92
Cornell Mountain 64
Craig Claire 48
Cramm, Gideon 24
Creek watcher 41-44, 57, 94
Crook, John 45
Cross Mountain Road 48
Cruickshank family 85
Cruickshank, Hiram 86
Crumbling, Allen 86-87
Cunningham 24

D

Davis, Elwyn 8
Decker, Jim 32, 45
Deep Hollow Notch 102
Delaware River 75
Delhi 93, 98, 106
Delhi Stage 92-93
DeSilva, Billy 20
DeSilva, Howard 20
DeSilva, Joe 40, 94
Dick, Charley 29
Double Top Mountain 72, 102
Downsville 92, 106
Drake, Aaron 73
Drinking, Mike's 35, 40, 65-66, 77-78, 88, 109, 113
Dry Brook 7-8, 11, 20, 22-24, 27, 32, 39-41, 52, 56-57, 78, 113
Dumond, Waldron 34, 36-38, 60, 63, 76-77, 81, 88, 90
Duryea, Commissioner 89-90
Dyeing 111
Dyer Hollow 85

E

Eagle Mountain 21, 76
Earle farm 26
East Branch 53, 61
East Deck 73
Easton 53
Eighteen-day hunt, see The Big Hunt
Ellenville 62

F

Factory 93
Fairbairn, Dave 78
Fairbairn, Frank 15, 30, 43, 47, 72, 97
Fairbairn, Robert 15, 19, 34
Fiddling 34-35
Finch, Jean Haynes 12
Fire jacks 62
Fish story 99
Flax 14
Fleischmann's Yeast 41

Fleischmann, Senator 42
Fleischmanns 15, 27, 41, 66
Folk Festival of the Catskill Mtns. 6
Folk museum 6-8
Ford, Charley 105
Forest rangers 104
Fox 83
French Woods 75
Furch, Leon 61
Furlough Lake 42-44, 101

G

Game laws 32, 42, 58
Game protectors or wardens 32, 40, 42, 58, 94, 104
Gavette, Elmer 30
Geneology 11-12
Genunge, Charlotte Haynes 11
Gevert, Rev. George 112
Ghost stories, see Spook stories
Gould estate 30, 33, 39, 42, 82
Gould, George 25, 39, 41, 101
Gould, Jay 101
Gould, Kingdon 89
Graham Mountain 22, 72-73, 102
Graham, Hiram 36, 47, 96
Graham, Will 26, 47
Granger, Mort, sons of 57
Green's Hotel, Roscoe 49
Green, George 42-44
Green, Will 47
Guitar 33

H

Hall, James G. 74
Hallenbeck 111
Hangbird's Nest 21
Hanson Eddy 53
Hardenburgh Patent 23
Harmonica 33-34
Haufrecht, Herbert 1
Haynes Hollow Road 87
Haynes, Betsy 14
Haynes, Claude 45
Haynes, George 83
Haynes, Grant 11
Haynes, Gwendolyn 86-87
Haynes, John 15-16, 19-20, 27, 29, 39, 44, 54, 63, 79
Haynes, Joseph 11, 24
Haynes, Judson 11
Haynes, Lena Knapp 23
Haynes, Nate 37, 79, 85
Haynes, Nina 58, 63, 81-82
Haynes, Ort 83
Highmount 26

INDEX

Hill, Gov. David B. 94, 104
Hilton, Dave 21, 105
Hobart 98
Hogan, Jack 103
Home remedies 53-54, 85
Homespun 15
Hoop making 17, 111
Hortonville 50
Howard, William G. 58, 89
Huckleberry industry 62
Hunt, Squire 24
Hunter 102
Hunter Mountain 93

J

Jews harp 33
Judson's Ridge 30

K

Keeney 89
Kelly, Ed 57
Kittle, Lou 83
Kittle, Bessie 23
Kittle, Edwin Hunt 23
Knapp, Charley 43-44
Knight, Jake 50
Knox, Henry Alexander etc. 65

L

Lackawack 8
Lambert, George 59, 107-109
Lambert, Mrs. George 109
Lawyers 89, 98-99
Lewis, Ed 66
Liddle, Mary 37
Linsey-woolsey 14
Little Hemlock Mountain 21
Livingston Manor 44, 61
Lon Dury Ridge 73
Lyons, Old Man 98-99

M

Margaretville 7, 18, 29, 66, 113
McGrath, Lawrence 60
Merwin, Mike's given name 11
Merwin, Samuel 24
Messenger, George 18
Milks, Benjamin 24
Millbook Road 90
Millbrook 8, 14, 47, 78
Millbrook Club 42
Ministers 97
Mitchell, Ephram 54
Moot's Dry Brook store 81
Moot, Jerome 81
Mount Burroughs 64

Mouth organ 34
Murphy, George C. 25
Murray Brook Hollow 107

N

Neighbors, a Camp Woodland periodical 6
Neversink River, East Branch 21, 80
Neversink River, West Branch 42, 75, 93, 104
No. 10 Hollow 108
Norwich 103

O

Old Forge 24-26
Old Mountain House 85
Oliverea 104
Oquago Creek 61
Outdoor Life, magazine 7

P

Palmer Hill 92
Palmer, Mrs. Clarence 114
Parker 96
Parson, George 85
Peekamoose Lake 80
Peekamoose Range 21
Pennybacker, Brink 56
Pension, Mike's 89-90
Pet snake 38
Phoenicia 3, 21
Pigeon Brook 72-73
Pine Hill 47
Poaching 31, 39-45
Polley, Cecil 37
Porcupines 63
Pranks 13, 79, 97
Prohibition 77

Q

Quillen, Boney 53

R

Rafting 52-55
Red Hill 80
Reed Swamp 102
Ruff, Old Man 42, 94
Revolutionary War 11
Rider Hollow 27, 76
Rondout Creek 80
Rose's Brook 39
Round Top Mountain 73
Roxbury 98

S

Sam's Point 62
Samuels, Sherwood 74

Saugerties 112
Scudder, Warren 25
Seager Valley 26
Seager, Uncle Murph 13, 15, 22-23, 25, 34, 37
Shacking 55
Shandaken 95
Shawangunk Mountains 62
Shingle shaving 17
Shoemaking 19
Skimmelton [Skimmerton] 96
Slide Mountain 64
Slide Mountain House 21
Smith, Beebe and Jack 44, 93-94
Smith, Mrs. Arthur 114
Snowshoe rabbits 63
Spinning 14
Spook stories 36
Springfield (army musket) 29
Spruce Mountain 22
Square dancing 4, 111
Square Elbow 102
Stagecoach Driver's Lad, The 8
Stagecoaches 91-92
Starr, Lee 114
Steel tempering 19
Steele, Undersheriff 25-26
Steer training 18
Stevens' Crack Shot (.22 rifle) 20
Stewart, George 44-45, 57
Stone laying 18, 51-52
Studer, Hannah 1
Sumansville 49
Sundown Road 80
Surveying 21-22

T

Tappan Road 23
Terry Clove 106
Todd Mountain 84
Todd, Burr 11
Todd, Charley 85
Todd, Charlotte (Lottie) 13, 16
Todd, Dyer, Mike's grandfather 11, 13, 96, 100
Todd, Elizabeth Genunge, Mike's mother 11, 14, 16, 113
Todd, Gerald 13, 16, 114

Todd, Hiram 47
Todd, Hiram Burr, Mike's father 11-13, 16-19, 23-25, 29-31, 33, 39-40, 47, 52, 79, 113
Todd, Ida 16
Todd, Jim 103-104
Todd, John 27
Todd, Judd 95
Todd, Ort, sons of 57
Todd, Rube 48, 101
Todd, Mrs. Russell 114
Todd, Samuel 11
Todd, Stratton 37, 58, 60
Tremperskill 25
Turner 101
Turnpikes 91
Turnwood 48-49
Twaddle Point 60-61
Tyler's 51
Tyler, Frank 105
Tyler, Nancy 55

U

Ulster & Delaware Railroad 40
Unadilla 98
Uncle Frank 28, 40, 48, 73

V

Van De Mark, Will 8
Van Kleeck, George 4, 111
Violin 33, 106

W

Walmsley, Will 48
Water witching 83-85
Watson Hollow 21
Weaving 15, 111
West, Ed 65, 77
Whalen, William 24
Willowemoc 32, 44-45, 75
Winnisook Lake 21, 64
Witches 36
Wittenberg Mountain 64
Woodland Valley 3, 64

Y

Yorks, Billy 73

Purple Mountain Press publishes books about New York State. For a free catalog, write: Purple Mountain Press, Ltd., P.O. Box E3, Fleischmanns, New York 12430-0378 or call: 914-254-4062 or fax: 914-254-4476 or e-mail: Purple@catskill.net.